Swedish
COUNTRY
INTERIORS

Swedish COUNTRY INTERIORS

RHONDA ELEISH & EDIE VAN BREEMS

Photography by Jon E. Monson & L. Langdon Ergmann

GIBBS SMITH
TO ENRICH AND INSPIRE HUMANKIND
Salt Lake City | Charleston | Santa Fe | Santa Barbara

First Edition
13 12 11 10 09   5 4 3 2 1

Text © 2009 Rhonda Eleish and Edie van Breems
Photographs © 2009 Jon E. Monson and L. Langdon Ergmann except for those on the following pages:
94-103 Peter Aaron/Esto Agency

Published by
Gibbs Smith
P.O. Box 667
Layton, Utah 84041

Orders: 1.800.835.4993
www.gibbs-smith.com
www.evbantiques.com

Designed and produced by Sheryl Dickert Smith and Maralee Nelson
Printed and bound in China
Gibbs Smith books are printed on either recycled, 100% post-consumer waste, FSC-certified papers or
on paper produced from a 100% certified sustainable forest/controlled wood source.

Library of Congress Cataloging-in-Publication Data

Eleish, Rhonda.
  Swedish country interiors / Rhonda Eleish and Edie van Breems. — 1st ed.
      p. cm.
  ISBN-13: 978-1-4236-0442-6
  ISBN-10: 1-4236-0442-3
  1. Interior decoration—Sweden. 2. Interior decoration—United States—Swedish influences. I. Van
Breems, Edie Bernhard. II. Title.
  NK2061.A1E43 2009
  747.09485—dc22
                        2009000471

This book is dedicated to my daughter, Kari.

My light; my blessing; my raison d'être.

—*Rhonda Eleish*

* e)*

With great love I dedicate this book to my father—
Van Bernhard. Seeker and builder of dreams, you are
nothing less than stanchion, brace, and buttress to mine.

—*Edie Bernhard van Breems*

CONTENTS

FOREWORD

LISA NEWSOM

I love Swedish style. When I was a child growing up in South Georgia, books and magazines were my windows on the world, and it was through them that I first discovered Sweden. In the beginning, I was drawn to the cooler colors: the greens of nature, the blues of sea and sky, the grays and off-whites of the winter season. That pristine Nordic look was completely different from my surroundings, and I was in its thrall. I still am.

Most of us think of Swedish style as simple, elegant Gustavian furnishings in spare rooms with pale colors that reflect light during long, dark days. This interior expression can be traced to King Gustav III, who reigned in Sweden from 1771 to 1792. He toured France and Italy, admired the classical style revival, and encouraged a distinctive Swedish interpretation of the look when he returned. I like to think of him as an editor like me, someone who reviews carefully and selects the best.

Over the years my appreciation has grown to embrace the warmer colors of Swedish dwellings and barns in the countryside painted the traditional Falun red or yellow ochre, the untreated wooden structures weathered a rich brown, and the heartfelt charm of folk art and furnishings.

In 2002, I visited Sweden for the first time and was transfixed. On that trip, all the images I held dear came to life in breathtaking beauty, and the people were gracious and welcoming. Lars Sjöberg, Sweden's passionate authority on eighteenth-century decorative arts, picked me up at my hotel to show me some of his nine restored historic houses. He was as casual as a next-door neighbor and had antique chairs strapped to the top of his Volvo. I realized he really represents the Swedes, from aristocrats to intellectuals to everyday folk, as egalitarian, relaxed, nature-loving people who don't like fussy furnishings, homes, or lives, but who seem to have innate good taste and style. Their way of looking at life resonates with many of us, and we create interiors reflecting that sensibility. Over the years, *Veranda* has featured many Swedish and Swedish-inspired interiors.

Rhonda Eleish and Edie van Breems, in their second book devoted to Swedish interiors, continue to share, through evocative images and knowledgeable text, their love of Swedish style from Gustavian to rustic. This book will become a cherished reference companion to their first, *Swedish Interiors.*

I have passed on my love of Sweden to my children. Their interiors, like so many today, vary from Continental to contemporary, but each incorporates Swedish antiques and colors in juxtapositions that are at once comfortable and sophisticated, reflecting that very special Swedish grace celebrated in this inspiring volume.

FOREWORD

DAVID EASTON

My first encounter with Swedish furniture was as a young designer. At that time, I had been to Europe on a scholarship and returned to work for Edward Wormley, a well-known furniture designer in New York City. Browsing one day at a neighborhood shop, Beekman Books, I found a three-volume set of books on classical Swedish furniture. These books, which I still have to this day, deeply impressed me, greatly affected my ideas about furniture design, and enriched my design soul. This prompted my travel to Sweden to see Swedish design firsthand.

Along the way, I had the chance to spend time with people who aided in my Swedish education. A wonderful friendship, both personal and professional, was with Merrill and Jan Stenbeck, clients whom I worked for in New York City and also on Long Island. I traveled down to their house in the Archipelago, where I met other friends and got to see their homes and the simple, yet elegant way that people lived in the countryside. When in Stockholm, I stayed at The Greenhouse, their wonderful hotel. Through Merrill and other friends, I met Lars Sjoberg, art historian, curator, and author. More recently, on a trip to Stockholm with friends, I revisited the Haga Pavilion, which was built in the seventeenth century by King Gustav III. The classical symmetry and simplicity of its design is timeless and ageless.

When King Gustav III made his grand tour through the courts of Europe, it left a lasting impression. Upon his return to Sweden, he, along with the architect Olof Tempelman, designer Louis Masreliez, and Swedish craftsmen, were responsible for creating this pavilion that adapts the grand style of the European courts. Its final effect is one of a comfortable,

charming, and more simple adaptation, appropriate to Sweden and the economy of the time. This translates well to the way we live now. My feeling about this small, delightful pavilion overlooking a lake is that it exemplifies the beauty and integration of Swedish architecture, decoration, and furnishings. It is as elegant in its provincial way as the period design created in France, Italy, and Russia. This principle of simplification of design also relates to the modern world we live in today.

Vitruvius, in the first century AD, said the principal ideals of great architecture were "commodity, firmness, and delight" (which can be translated as functionality, structural integrity, and aesthetic value). These principles still hold true, and Swedish furnishings and architecture exemplify these ideals.

Swedish furniture is unique and that is due to its simplification of detail, softer lines, simple wood, and painted finishes. This simplification of form and finish makes it equally as beautiful as any piece of furniture that the Continental or Russian courts and craftsmen created during the same period.

In this age of metal, glass, and concrete, it is important to draw upon the past to understand how it affects the way we live and design our homes today. What is relevant to design today is the simple elegance of Swedish style. As Mies van der Rohe said at the beginning of the twentieth century, "less is more" and that is exactly why Swedish furniture does not lose its appeal.

The homes that are featured in *Swedish Country Interiors* illustrate how universal and adaptive the Swedish style is. There is an enduring, timeless quality of the simple Swedish style that continues to speak to us all today.

PREFACE

Welcome! *Swedish Interiors*, our first book, was an overview of the history of Swedish design and how various homeowners and designers have been inspired to use those design elements in their homes. In this book, we are thrilled to have the opportunity to delve further into one style of Swedish design—Swedish country interiors—a subject most close to our hearts. As antiques dealers specializing in Swedish eighteenth- and nineteenth-century furnishings, we have had the pleasure to travel Sweden extensively. In our journeys over the past ten years, we have found ourselves not only inspired but fascinated by the strong beauty of antique Swedish country furnishings and the rhythms of a long-ago way of life. Interviews with Swedish farmers, reminiscences with elderly Swedish relatives, research at the Nordic Museum, and visits to Skansen (Stockholm's open-air museum) served to whet our appetites for more knowledge of Swedish country furnishings and design. Before we knew it, we had become obsessed with not just furniture but every dust-covered tool we stumbled upon from this vibrant pre-twentieth-century flax-and-milk-based culture. We spent long hours hand-mixing pigment paints and learning the secrets, frustrations, and joys of working with natural Swedish materials as we attempted to incorporate what we had seen in Sweden into our own homes and our store, Eleish Van Breems Antiques.

In writing this book we have looked back and considered why the country traditions in particular held so much appeal for us. The stunning formal Gustavian furniture of the cities is what had originally lured us to buy furniture in Sweden, but we clearly had fallen under the spell of the *allmoge*, a word that translates to "folk" or "of the people." We both had homes of our own in the Connecticut countryside with children, husbands, and animals to tend to, so one might infer that we found the idea of farm living intellectually relatable. However, it is precisely the differences between our world and that of the Swedish country house that captured our attention. We were truly humbled and in awe of a people who were in tune with the rhythms of nature, and we admired their inventive mastery of precious native materials.

As we began to speak with other collectors and admirers of both provincial and peasant Swedish country style, we were struck by how the Swedish country way of life and the practical yet exciting hallmarks of Swedish eighteenth- and nineteenth-century decoration are touch points that we could incorporate into our own homes. In *Swedish Country Interiors*, you will find numerous examples of Swedish country living that the homeowners in this book have embraced and from which they have derived inspiration including wall decorations, functional furnishings, natural upholstery materials, use of light, and indoor-outdoor living, to name but a few. Although we are devoted antiquarians, our interest is not in showing pristine pastiches of Swedish folk interiors. What excites us is the opportunity to share how various homeowners live today in our very own countryside and city suburbs, blending within their contemporary homes the very best that Swedish country lifestyle and design has to offer. We thank each one of them for sharing their individual love affairs with Sweden and for allowing us to present the unique beauty of their homes with the world beyond their welcoming garden gates.

—*Edie & Rhonda*

FACING: A nineteenth-century Bavarian armoire (circa 1800) looks beautiful next to a nineteenth-century Swedish Gustavian-style bench (circa 1860).

INTRODUCTION

THE PAST AND FUTURE

The pines are individuals, full of wind and song,
Of crossing and storm, of character and purposeful
Aspiration. They are more venerable than ourselves.
Timber are trees, which life has become a fairytale.
To build walls of th is to close yourself indoors with
your conscience between antiquity and future.

—Lars Israel Wahlman

Though simple, seventeenth- and eighteenth-century Swedish homesteads were, by most European traveler's accounts from the period, fairly hospitable dwellings. One of the most famous visitors to Sweden, whose name we still recognize today, is the British writer Mary Wollstonecraft. In her 1796 essay, "A Short Residency in Sweden," she tells us of a Swedish stuga: "On entering, I was still better pleased to find a clean house, with some degree of rural elegance. The beds were of muslin, coarse is true, but dazzling white; and the floor was strewed over with all the sprigs of juniper (the custom as I afterwards found of the country), which formed a contrast with the curtains and produced an agreeable sensation of freshness, to soften the ardor of noon. Still nothing was as pleasing as the alacrity of hospitality—all of what the house afforded was quickly spread on the whitest linen."

The home Wollstonecraft entered was typical of the rural class of Sweden. We must turn our eyes to the heart and hearths of these farmers' homesteads in order to fully understand the true origins of Swedish Country design and the

indomitable spirit from which it sprang. Records tell us that in 1871 four-fifths of the Swedish population was agricultural. This rural agricultural worker is often referred to in European writings as a "peasant" but in Swedish the word used is *bonder*, which means "dwellers." Sometimes the bonder would own the farm they worked on, but most often they would hold a lease from the crown or another owner. Another lower level of agricultural worker was the cottar, who would rent a small plot of ground and keep a few animals. These people would work during the harvest for their richer neighbors.

Most of a bonder's life in the country was one of hard work punctuated by seasonal celebrations; hospitality and entertaining in the home were rare occasions to look forward to. Most of spring and summer life focused on the livestock and farming. By the end of the eighteenth century, due to increasingly harsh land laws and taxation, many farmers found that they could not subsist without another source of income. During the long winter months, many made all sorts of useful decoratively carved items. In some provinces, such as Dalecarlia, peasants would

FACING: This Connecticut living room is the epitome of what we define as Swedish high country style. A rococo Swedish pine settee is upholstered in blue checked gingham and sits facing a Gustavian tea table with a faience top dating from circa 1770.

travel down to outlying cities to sell the wares they had made in the winter. All manner of baskets, wooden bowls, linens, and lace were brought to market. Among the many other items to be carved and decorated were wooden horse collars, harness saddles and pins, wooden scutching knives, hand mangles, and batlets. Often these were carved with birds, hearts, flowers, and ancient starburst motifs, usually to be given by grooms as tokens of affection to their brides.

Marriage was the one great event in Swedish peasant life, and preparation for it was taken very seriously. Almost every region of Sweden had its own customs surrounding the ceremony. In the province of Skåne, for example, elaborately embroidered carriage cushions were made with the couple's initials set into the design. Marriage armoires from northern towns such as Ångermanland were elaborately carved and always painted with the couple's initials and date of marriage. In the farming area around Lake Siljan, copper ceremonial milking buckets with lavish initial and floral designs were a common gift. Maidens all over Sweden would spend most of their youth weaving and knitting their dowry as it was all they took with them from their old life. Trunks were prepared and usually decoratively painted and, in wealthier homes, this dowry could be comprised of many lavish trunks, livestock, and even land. This furniture and other items remain both powerful and charming examples of Swedish folk art.

By the middle of the eighteenth century, painted decorations had spread to the furnishings and walls of the home. Communities looked forward to religious holidays with great anticipation for the social aspect of bringing together community. Painted wall and ceiling hangings, usually depicting biblical stories, were made for such special occasions. During Christmas, Easter, weddings, and christenings, these painted "tapestries" would be brought out and the table would be set with the finest linens and serving dishes of the household. Wealthier farms would have a room for entertaining, which would be heated and set with a banquet table and an area just for music and dancing.

In the South of Sweden, where *stugas* were generally designed with long ridgepoles running through the center of the building, decorative woven tapestries were hung from the poles and ceilings. These tapestries have their roots as far back as the Viking age. In the mid-eighteenth century came the development of the *bonad*, or ceiling tapestry, which was not a textile so much as a canvas. *Bonads* were long strips of linen, often several yards long, covered in a gesso and decoratively painted with various biblical stories; the characters depicted are most often dressed in contemporary Swedish garb. *Bonads* are said to originate from journeymen artists Anders Sillman and Peter Edbergmen in South Unnaryd in 1763. They passed on their skills to a local, Nils Lindberg, who became the founder of the Unnaryd School. Johannes Nilsson (1757–1827) is the most famous of the *bonad* painters from this school. As court painters used engravings from France as inspiration for their painted palace interiors, so the country *bonad* painters used German engravings and fashion plates as stylistic templates for their colorful, whimsical paintings.

In the North, in the region of Dalarna, where building styles did not lend themselves to *bonad*, wall canvases were the vogue. Dala painting developed in two very distinct styles—the Rättvik school and the Leksand school. A third, looser style was found to the west of the Dala River. These styles or schools refer not just to wall paintings but also to the furniture that was decoratively painted to match the walls. Of the Leksand school, the best-known paintings are the flower depictions of Carl Winter Hansson and the work of Back Eric Andersson. The Rättvik school, founded by Eric Eliasson, was more subdued. These paintings used darker colors but covered every surface with pattern. Painters from the area of Lima, most famously Hallars Mattias Hansson (1778–1871), are noted for leaving on the walls, trunks, and armoires that they painted a distinct blue rectangular shape for initials or dates and large, round rose-like flowers. Ultimately, in regions such as Dalarna, where folk art became a commodity, the painting became stylized because the

Ceremonial rakes like these were used to rake the piles of flax silk.

painters began to work quickly. Sometimes patterns on furniture, in lesser hands, became simplified beyond recognition.

The colorful and exuberant style of Swedish peasant decoration would, over the years, meet head-on with the formal French-inspired Gustavian style of the court of Gustav III. A provincial version of Gustavian style can most often be found in manor houses, wealthier farms, merchant houses, and homes of Swedish mine owners and managers. Painters who had been apprentices and had trained with court painters in Stockholm found their way out to the countryside. To have your house interior painted by one of them was a sign of prestige. The

dark red-, black-, and ochre-painted furniture typical of the baroque and rococo periods in the Swedish countryside was slowly abandoned for furniture painted in the soft pearl grays, blues, and yellows of the Gustavian court. The love of warm colors and decoration was the older tradition of country decorating. The new Gustavian style, with its cooler palette, began to slowly filter into the countryside, resulting in an equally unique type of country interior.

At the turn of the century, technological innovation brought change to the decoration of Swedish country houses. Nineteenth-century colored prints from Brandenburg, Germany, started to arrive in Sweden and soon drove hand-painted wall hangings out of the market amongst the peasantry. Wall

hangings, once the domain of only the richest peasant, became mass-market items and, unfortunately, with mass production came a total degeneration of the art form. Paper was used instead of fabric, and cruder colors and drawing distinguish some of these late examples. George Karlin of the Museum of Kulturen in Lund sums it up best when he writes, "By 1830s peasant taste was abandoned. The hungry and thirsting artistic sense had to eat and drink itself full on lithographs from Neuruppin and as many oleographs as the wall could hold."

By the turn of the century, the industrialization that started the decline of traditional living in the countryside—from mass-produced furniture to cheap factory-made textiles— sparked concern among a number of select Swedish intellectuals and artists. Widespread migration to the cities and abroad during the famines of the 1860s furthered the decline. In this regard, Sweden was similar to England where members of its Arts and Crafts movement were interested in preserving England's own disappearing traditions. The Swedish movement during this time would come to be known as the Swedish Romantic movement. Fearing that the country's many customs, architecture, and native handcrafted arts would be irreparably lost

to history, teacher and ethnologist Artur Hazelius founded the Nordic Museum in 1872. Hazelius also bought up examples of Swedish buildings all across Sweden and brought them to Stockholm's Djurgargen, where in 1891 he opened Skansen, the world's first open-air museum.

A rising middle class was exposed to Skansen, and the ideal of a simpler way of life in the country was something that city dwellers began to romanticize. Swedes began to build summerhouses and pavilions, emulating the tradition of summer retreats set forth by the aristocrats. With many of the rural farms having been left empty or for sale during the migration of the 1860s, it was possible to buy and restore these old timber buildings. Add to that the success of artists Carl and Karin Larsson's books on their home in Sundborn and the Swedish country home as a friendly place, and Swedish country style became fixed in the national psyche as a retreat to a simpler time and a place to connect with nature.

Freestanding cupboards like this one were used to display wooden plates, spoons, ceramics, and pewter.

Today we look at the origins of Swedish country interiors of the eighteenth and nineteenth centuries in order to gain perspective on the past as well as to give us a view towards the future. What exactly does Swedish country interiors mean today? Swedish country, in our century, can be rustic, rural, urban, comfortable, family friendly, elegant, simple, complex, grand, humble, and eclectic. Simply put, Swedish country interiors involve a wide spectrum of interpretations.

Hallmarks of Swedish country style include folk-painted tall case clocks and painted furniture, checked ginghams and crisp white linens, pickled wood floors, and an abundance of light in interior spaces.

Ultimately, however, Swedish country is really more about lifestyle design. Swedish lifestyle is a natural way of living including clean uncluttered spaces and drawing on local building materials. The inclusion of natural exterior elements in interiors is standard practice in Swedish design.

The appreciation and respect for nature is ever present in daily Swedish life. It is no surprise then that Swedish interiors reflect that. Maintaining symmetry between indoors and outdoors is accomplished by the use of pleasing, softer colors; the

use of natural light where possible; and the elimination of busy clutter to create positive space. In the land of the midnight sun, where summer light is savored and the winters are long and dark, it is understandable why natural light is cherished. In essence, Swedish-influenced interior design is firstly based on nature, secondly on structure.

Design is always about evolution, and it is apparent that the word *country* has evolved. A common perspective is shared; however, the interpretations vary greatly. There is no such thing as one style of Swedish country. In these pages, we have traveled around the United States and share with you the wonderful homes we have had the pleasure to visit. Some interiors reflect a more formal approach to country, some a more rustic. However, the common thread these homeowners share is a love and desire to live the lifestyle of Swedish design.

Blondell's in Minnesota has a collection of allmoge furniture that is most typical to the area north of Stockholm. All of the furniture pictured is made of pine and was painted by eighteenth- and nineteenth-century regional artisans and farmers using natural mineral pigment paints.

SWEDISH MEDITERRANEAN

THE PALO ALTO HOME OF CHERIE AND MICHAEL MCKINNEY

*D*riving down a redwood- and sycamore-lined street near downtown Palo Alto, California, one is surprised to come upon an enchanted Swedish birch grove with underplantings of fern and the sounds of a babbling brook. Through the birch trees, above a walled courtyard, one can glimpse a cheery yellow house with a red tile roof and blue-and-white windows. The house registers as both Mediterranean and Northern European at the same time. "I've always loved Swedish interiors," says owner Cherie McKinney. "My great, great grandparents, Johannes and Greta Hansson, emigrated from Sweden to Minnesota, and their son, John Alfred, then homesteaded in Montana, but it's funny how no one else in the family was very connected to that part of our Swedish American heritage." Cherie's dream was to bring Swedish interiors into this very Spanish Revival house, and over the years she and her husband, Michael, have assembled an ace triumvirate of architect, interior designer, and landscape architect to do just that.

FACING: The interior designer for the home had salmon-checked slipcovers made for the Swedish rococo-style side chairs to give the dining room a more relaxed country feeling. The slipcovers are easily removed to reveal the more formal aqua-colored velvet-upholstered cushions underneath.

LEFT: Natural light highlights Cherie's eighteenth-century tray table. The blue-and-white Rörstrand faience top is supported by cabriole legs. The pine tray table is painted brown to imitate a more valuable wood such as mahogany.

ABOVE: An eighteenth-century three-drawer Swedish buffet dominates one end of the dining room. Above the dado, a wall mural of painted panels draped with floral garlands adds architectural interest to a simple wall. Painters Jonas and Stephan derived inspiration from the light floral garlands eighteenth-century Swedish painter Lars Bolander painted at another grand Swedish house, Sturehov Manor. Roses and peonies from Cherie's garden tumble from a pewter vase, echoing the exuberance of the painted blooming garlands.

LEFT: Swedish crystal chandeliers dazzle and add a light and airy feel to any room.

FACING: Designer Suzanna Havden Bell chose two Swedish chandeliers in the style of Olaf Westerberg to hang in the living room. Groupings of chandeliers in drawing rooms are traditional to manor houses and palaces throughout Sweden, with up to four chandeliers hanging from painted baroque ceilings in houses such as Beatelund.

"When Cherie and Michael bought the house, it was still a cottage with no second story, so you can see that the addition has been quite large," says their architect Howard Bankston Post. "What was interesting about this project for me was that a client usually has only a vague sense of the direction they want to go in, but Cherie was different in that she was an irresistible force—she had a very specific visualization." Cherie nods and adds with a laugh, "We made a diabolic team because we are both such perfectionists!" Cherie was passionate about sourcing the right building materials and soon found old-growth heart pine flooring salvaged from the Wadley Building in Georgia; French and English antique stone was also found; even Makkum Delft tiles from Holland were imported. The house lacked spacial organization, so it was decided that pilaster and beams were to be added along a central spine, including through the living room. Windows and French doors were installed to allow light throughout the day, and a master bedroom suite was added as well as an office and entertainment room. With the structural renovations complete, the McKinneys focused on the surrounding property.

Landscape architect Jim Chadwick is known for creating integrated elements of stone, rock, and wood that are synergistic with his plantings and trees. Jim was introduced to the McKinney project and imparted a Swedish feeling to the grounds, planting woodland flora and birch trees, incorporating boulders, and installing water features such as fountains and rills. In keeping with the Northern mystique, a water feature running beneath the bedroom window evokes all the sounds of a forest stream. "Cherie and Michael love their flower and vegetable gardens," states Jim. "And to that end, we will continue to add very Northern European garden features; for example, right now we are nurturing along an eighty-foot bed planted with espaliered fruit trees to grow among the California lemons."

ABOVE: The fireplace was moved to this interior wall during the renovation. The rustic nineteenth-century wooden milk pan on the mantel is a reminder of the central importance of food and hearth in the traditional pre-twentieth-century Swedish home. The milk pan, painted Falun red, also picks up the color and rusticity of the Swedish trunk used as a coffee table.

FACING: Soft tones of blue continue upstairs in the bedroom, where a rare 1770s tea table sits between two comfortable armchairs.

With the house and garden in place, Cherie turned to working on the details that would make the home feel more Swedish. "I loved the Swedish look, I was drawn to it—it was just something inside of me," says Cherie. "But during the renovation, I started to become frustrated about being able to achieve the look." What she was struggling to find was just the right yellow for the exterior of the house and trying to replicate a painted dado from a Swedish castle. It was at this

point that Cherie discovered The Swedish Room and its owner, Swedish interior designer Suzanna Havden Bell. Located in the Sobell Design Building in the San Francisco Design Center, Bell's showroom deals in fine Swedish reproduction furniture and antiques. Here was the person who would be able to bring Cherie's vision to the next level.

"The first thing I noticed when I entered the house was all of the marvelous light, and Cherie and I decided on colors based

ABOVE: The breakfast room table is lit by a massive nineteenth-century Swedish chandelier. Cherie readily uses her French Quimper collection and Souleiado linens in this traditional Swedish dining area. The slat-back chairs are known as Leksand chairs and are a very traditional yet modern form found in most Swedish houses. Suzanna added comfortable cushions made of check gingham to the chairs. The small Dalarna cupboard, dated 1845, would have been used to hold the Bible and other precious objects. Traditionally, the master's chair or bridal chair would be placed under the cupboard as a place of honor reserved for the head of the household or a special guest.

FACING, ABOVE: Cherie's Swedish cupboard, set in the hallway, is dated 1843 and is of a provincial style. The furniture painter used forceful, almost abstract graining techniques to suggest a rustic mahogany. The form of the cupboard is traditional to the baroque period; so well loved was this furniture form that examples were still being made in Sweden well into the nineteenth century.

FACING, BELOW: The white-plastered hearth in the breakfast room is reminiscent of those found in Swedish *stugas*. Here, instead of an open cook space, the fire is closed off with a brass-and-glass fire screen. A pair of armchairs based on those found at Gripsholm invite one to sit. Swedish style meets California living with warmth and texture coming from the terra-cotta tiles.

on keeping the mood soft and airy," says Suzanna. "Of course the renovation had almost been completed when I came on the scene, but I was able to help out with a few Swedish details." Among those were the plaster texture, the paneling, and helping Jim Chadwick design Swedish fretwork balustrades for the deck and a heavy wooden gate. It was necessary to pick just the right tone for the interior paint colors. Cherie had found a great source for paint—the Sydney Harbor Paint Company, whose paint had just the right texture and quality for achieving the Swedish look and feel—but to Suzanna's eye, the color tones were too pastel. She added pigment—mostly grays—to achieve the perfect tone, and the paint company was then able to match her hand-mixed colors.

Reproducing an authentic Swedish floor that met with Suzanna's satisfaction was even more challenging. "We had to work very hard on samples back and forth until my finisher finally got the appearance of the natural-looking scrubbed floors that are so typical of Sweden. The secret," reveals Suzanna, "is to bleach the floors just the right amount of times to remove the yellow without taking the life out of the wood. A hand-mixed selection of pigments is then applied with the goal to maintain the light but at the same time give depth to achieve that natural worn look to the wood. The floors turned out to be absolutely beautiful."

"I'm very happy with the result, and it made my and Cherie's stubbornness about getting it just right so worth it!" says Suzanne.

To add interest to the rooms, Suzanna also suggested including wall murals, which provided Swedish flair. "Cherie was the perfect candidate for wall murals," notes Suzanna, "as she had long admired them while browsing through her Swedish decorating

ABOVE: A window seat in the office invites one to sit and view the gardens and terraces.

FACING: This tree-peony mural that Suzanna has installed in the front entrance hall was inspired by Tree of Life wallpaper from the minute-but-dramatic Prima Donna's dressing room at the Drottningholm Court Theatre. Sweden, like much of Europe, was taken with all things Chinese, and the 1770s wallpaper is a Swedish interpretation of Chinese textiles.

books, and her walls were perfectly prepped for them." Wall canvases depicting all manner of dado, paneling, and moldings have been used in Swedish interiors since baroque times. The vogue for these panels, usually depicting curling tendrils of flowers or foliage hung in garland swags, reached its height in the 1760s to 1780s. Renowned Swedish painters Jonas Wickman and Stephan Söder continue this tradition today and were specially flown in from Stockholm by Suzanna to paint Cherie's murals.

With the flooring and walls done properly and a color palette set, Cherie and Suzanna were able to turn towards procuring the fabrics and furniture. Antiques were handpicked and the reproduction furniture was all made and custom hand-

finished in Sweden. Fine details can be found throughout the house, from the hand-smithed wrought iron hardware made in a small Swedish village to the built-in cabinetry designed by Suzanna to add Swedish charm and functionality in Cherie and Michael's office.

"We used only the best in Cherie's house. I always say that the basics are so important. If you invest in classic, quality materials and select neutral soft finishes for your base and take the time to develop your ideas, you will be content with your home for many years," states Suzanna. "In Sweden, they build their homes over many years, by inheriting an antique chest from a relative, by picking up art from one of their travels in Europe, or by finding a great chandelier at

a flea market. Still, so many Swedes have beautiful, charming homes. Being a Swede myself," continues Suzanna, "I feel
odd saying that Swedes have a great sense of style, but it's
really true. Or is it simply because your home reflects you
as a person and each one of those pieces has a story to tell?
Each piece is unique and different, and building a home is
a process that involves handpicking what you have passion
for and making it work. This is my motto, and this is why I
enjoyed working with Cherie so much—she has those same
values and shares my huge passion for beautiful things. The
McKinney's house has really evolved over the course of a few
years and will continue to evolve for Cherie and Michael over
many more to come." ❋

FACING: Cherie's cupboard holds her remarkable collection of antique
Swedish linens. This eighteenth-century cupboard was over painted at some
point, a common occurrence in Sweden. Enough of the original blue paint
shows through to tease Cherie into thinking she may restore it one day back
to its original glory.

ABOVE: Landscape architect Jim Chadwick created a Scandinavian glade on
the front side of the house, complete with fern and lupine. The yellow color
of the house was inspired by the Stromsholm Palace. "When you see Cherie
and Michael's house," says Suzanna, "you get a sense of happiness. It's
always sunshine over at the McKinney's."

THE SWEDISH MILL HOUSE

THE BERKSHIRE RETREAT OF EDITH GILSON

*M*usic, art, and cultural energy are what originally drew Cupboards & Roses Antiques owner Edith

Gilson to the Berkshires. While working in the city in 1984, Edith began her quest for a weekend house that was

an escape from the madness of the corporate world. As a respected businesswoman, her opinions were published

in the *New York Times* advertising section and in major trade publications in the U.S. and abroad. Edith, a senior

vice president of J. Walter Thompson Agency and author of *Unnecessary Choices*, an in-depth study of American

women at the top of the corporate ladder, soon found the perfect property, which, in many ways, reminded her of

her childhood in Bavaria.

unpainted
15 - trex

FACING: Originally a working paper mill in the nineteenth century, the factory has been elegantly transformed into a beautiful interior as well as exterior space.

LEFT: The terrace overlooks the river that once powered the White Paper Mill.

The color-pigmented plaster that was used for the living room was inspired by the buildings of Vienna, Austria. The color is soft and warm, perfect for creating an intimate feel in a larger space. Edith also chose not to include window treatments in the main living space so that the maximum amount of light could be absorbed into the room. This decision was inspired by the Swedish interior sensibility of natural light and letting nature in.

In keeping with Edith's desire to keep her home livable, she mixed contemporary soft seating in homespun fabrics with fine eighteenth- and nineteenth-century Swedish antiques. A pair of small stools (Sweden, circa 1880) in the Gustavian style, and a nineteenth-century Swedish tall case clock stand out as fine examples.

This gray-and-white tall case clock from Jämtland, Sweden (circa 1790), with original Norwegian soapstone weights, is one of the exquisite antiques that Edith has collected. The carved crown with flowers and foliage is particularly unique and a fine example of a clock that came from a well-established home in eighteenth-century Sweden. To quote Edith, her love of Swedish tall case clocks stems from their form: "Swedish tall case clocks are feminine, where the English tall case clock is very masculine. The Swedish clocks make you want to smile." This particular clock looks like a regal queen.

Built in 1850 as the original mill house for the White Paper Factory, the structure had spacious rooms, high ceilings, and the perfect location right on the river, all of which Edith immediately fell in love with. The building needed extensive work, as did the property, to establish it as a living space; however, Edith, so enchanted, was not fazed.

While she commuted and worked on the house during the weekends, she soon began to realize that she was making up any excuse to stay at the house for one extra day rather than return to New York City. Thus, the process of self-examination began. After she had determined that she had achieved all that she wanted to in the world of advertising, Edith decided it was time for her to make a change in her life. The Berkshires felt like home, so it was there she stayed.

What was the next step? As a teenager in Europe, Edith had hitchhiked throughout Scandinavia and had always remembered a grace and wonderful sense of elegance in that area of the world. She carried those impressions with her into her adult life, and when the decision to start a new career was made, her earlier impressions became vital to her new venture. In 1989, she opened the doors to Cupboards & Roses Antiques, and she never looked back.

Cupboards & Roses specializes in beautiful, original painted antiques from Edith's childhood home of Bavaria as well as original antiques from Scandinavia, particularly Sweden.

According to Edith, she loves going to Sweden and Scandinavia and feels very at home there. She admires the elegance of the style, which is not too polished. She fell in love with the contradiction between the elegant form and the painted surface. Brown furniture had never been a part of Edith's design aesthetic. Childhood influences of painted Bavarian interiors as well as a natural sense for the beautiful simplicity of Swedish style had always been the guiding design force in her life.

When designing her retail space in Sheffield, Massachusetts, Edith referred back to her mill house for inspiration. Her home is for living and entertaining, and Edith wanted her store to reflect a similar feel. Spacious and grand, yet understated and elegant, the store makes one instantly feel welcomed and relaxed. One also feels the passion of the collector. After eighteen years, Edith is still excited to do what she does. Each piece has a personality, each trip has a story.

This very rare Swedish *bonad* (watercolor on paper), dated 1821, painted by Hakan Karisson, and showing the regiment on parade, is part of Edith's treasured collection. Cupboards & Roses specializes in rare and unique folk art such as the Swedish *bonad* drawings.

According to Edith, the Swedish word *bonad* means simply "wall hanging." The *bonads* at Cupboards & Roses Antiques are from the south of Sweden and date from about 1650 to the middle of the nineteenth century. They might be considered the "poor man's tapestry." Painted on paper, burlap, or hemp, they were hung or attached to the walls of the main room, bringing color and a touch of elegance to small, dark interiors.

Whimsical touches in living spaces, as well as contemporary art, contribute to creating a sense of eclectic elegance. A Swedish toy horse (circa 1890) stands tall, a modern painting by acclaimed African American artist Romare Bearden tells a story, and zinc ornaments add architectural depth.

The Bearden, according to Edith, "is oil on paper and was given to me long before he became well known. Additionally, the work between the two windows is a portrait of me by my sister, Ursula Roos—*Edith in New England Autumn*, watercolor and pencil on paper."

Nineteenth-century rare shield-back Gustavian-style side chairs surround an English nineteenth-century gateleg tavern table (one of the first antiques Edith ever purchased). A Swedish sideboard from the later Gustavian period (circa 1810), in white paint, and a pair of carved and gilded wood mirrors from the Karl Johan, or empire, period (Sweden, circa 1830) create a charming and well-balanced mix of dark and light surfaces that is also repeated in the kitchen.

ABOVE: An enclosed porch overlooking the river is yet another space where life is enjoyed and friends and family are welcome.

FACING: A pair of black-painted nineteenth-century Swedish armchairs in the rococo style (circa 1880) flanks a rare eighteenth-century Swedish baroque black granite-top table (circa 1740). The painting of blue lilies, a treasured item in Edith's house, was painted for her by artist Ellen Lanyon. All of the art displayed in Edith's home was given to her by visiting artists and friends. Her home is truly dedicated to her family, friends, and enjoying life.

ABOVE: An early Swedish rococo game table (circa 1760) sits perfectly next to a primitive nineteenth-century Swedish faux bois chest of drawers (circa 1840) from Dalarna, Sweden.

FACING: One of Edith's most treasured pieces is the early American "Edith" hook rug that was given to her by a dear friend right before she underwent major surgery a few years ago. It is a symbol of her speedy recovery and a constant reminder to enjoy life.

Utilizing local and indigenous materials to build is environmentally friendly as well as very Swedish. Ways of building that do not tax the environment are supported as well as encouraged in Sweden. When building the kitchen interior, Edith called upon her cabinetmaker to construct cabinets made from the wood of a local cherry tree of her neighbor's across the river.

As a contrast to the warm cherry tones, Edith kept strictly to tonal whites when choosing her dishes, pottery, and kitchen accessories. Because she decided to keep the top cabinets open for convenience and keep the shelving white, the choice of white accessories was practical as well as visually appealing. A sense of balance and order was maintained with little color introduced.

Again, to offset the warmer tones of the cabinets, Edith introduced a set of eighteenth-century Swedish Gustavian centennial dining chairs (circa 1780) with wheat sheaf carving on the splats, and covered the dining table with a white nineteenth-century Swedish quilt.

The gilt "E," as well as the other "E" letters in the house, were given to Edith on various visits by friends and family.

FACING: In a corner of the library, an eighteenth-century vignette transports the visitor to another time and place. The corner chair, a rare find, is eighteenth-century Swedish rococo (circa 1760) with its original blue paint, and the eighteenth-century Swedish tilt-top table is from the same period. Notice the feet of the tilt-top table—the form was derived from an English Queen Anne base.

ABOVE: When restoring the mill house, Edith thought it would be in keeping to incorporate an original worktable from the factory as part of the décor. Once a factory work surface in the 1850s, the table now serves as an entertainment pause point.

RIGHT: This *bonad* (Edith has nicknamed them "the women") is a wonderful example from Edith's personal collection. A fragment of an 1840 Swedish *bonad*, it is painted tempera on paper, showing five figures in period dress. Edith chose to frame the *bonad* in a formal frame because she liked the play between contrasts. In her opinion, some of the most interesting *bonads* that she has collected have been fragments as opposed to complete scenes.

ABOVE: An early nineteenth-century Swedish secretary (circa 1800), a pair of eighteenth-century Swedish baroque demi-lune tables (circa 1740) in original paint, and a collection of nineteenth-century American blue-painted buckets on a bench are displayed with elegant simplicity.

LEFT: Fine examples of a bridal *bonad* (circa 1860) from the private collection of Edith Gilson.

FACING: A nineteenth-century Bavarian armoire (circa 1800) looks beautiful next to a nineteenth-century Swedish Gustavian-style bench (circa 1860).

NEW HAMPSHIRE ISLAND LIVING

THE COTTAGE OF THE LORD AND HOLSTEN FAMILIES

Situated on one of the two hundred and forty-four islands in the heart of New Hampshire's Lake Winnipesaukee lies the summer lake house of the Holsten and Lord families. When it came time to build a summer cottage, Chris Lord and Gretel Holsten didn't have to look far for a location; both families had been coming to the island since the 1950s. Traditionally in Sweden, summer homes are where families holiday together and generations mix. Chris and Gretel felt strongly about keeping that tradition alive for their two sons, Christopher and George, and before they knew it, the opportunity arrived.

FACING: An early-nineteenth-century Swedish tall case clock flanks the corner of the living room. Libby Holsten, designer and Gretel's mother, loved the hints of original terra-cotta and sage paint detailed on the surface. She added an American primitive chair as an anchor for the clock.

Gretel's son Christopher came home one day from school with a Dala horse constructed of twigs that he had gathered. Above the sculpture hangs an oil painting on board, which belonged to Libby's mother. The painting and Christopher's horse present the perfect Swedish composition.

LEFT: The island provides ample opportunities for the family to spend long days by the water.

As luck would have it, they were able to acquire the last lot left on their desired side of the island with a view to the White Mountains, and the project to clear the land began. The planning and construction of the lake house was a pure labor of love and took five years to complete. All building materials had to travel by barge; therefore, construction was limited due to seasonal challenges. Contractor Paul Borders of Island Services Corporation rigged a boat trailer with a sledlike base to enable the builders to bring lumber to the site during the winter months. The process still took weeks, but finally construction was able to begin.

In keeping with the idea of a special place for family and of keeping tradition alive for the next generation, Gretel Holsten's father, George Holsten, a Massachusetts physician, contributed greatly to making the lake house a reality. The Holsten family had had a house on the island for generations, and George felt passionately about establishing a summer home for the next generation.

Now that the land was cleared, Chris enlisted his brother, Jonathan Lord, a landscape designer and architectural draftsman, to help design the project. Jonathan created a design inspired by homes that both families liked, specifically where all rooms faced the water. The families also sought input from architect and family friend Jim Malcolm. In planning, the main request that Gretel had was that the kitchen be equipped with a walk-in pantry. Although a nurse by profession, Gretel's

passion is her love of the culinary arts, and because island living can be logistically difficult, Gretel wanted to make sure that she would be able to store food long term.

George wanted to work within the island's environment to create the island's only well. Despite the great challenge of finding someone willing and capable of drilling through nearly 300 feet of solid rock ledge, George's vision resulted in a well providing the home with enough water to run efficiently. As a result of traffic on the lake, the island's water quality has been compromised over the years; therefore, the well is a source of pure water for the family.

With the lake house construction well underway, Gretel called on her mother, antiques dealer and designer Libby Holsten, for interior inspiration. The lake house is a seasonal residence with no central heat—

FACING: The lakeside hammock provides a quiet resting spot for summer naps.

ABOVE: During the design phase of the house, Jim Malcolm designed a deck that appears to be floating, creating a symbiotic flow to the house. Throughout the summer months, the family uses the deck daily.

just a wood-burning stove—and Libby drew on the creative energy from the summer homes of Sweden to inspire her. Not unlike the many island summer homes in Sweden, this house maintains a natural sense of balance in its environment.

The pale pickled walls were chosen as a reaction to the dark house interiors of lake houses that Gretel and Chris were familiar with while growing up; the pale walls were also an ode to Libby's love of Scandinavian interiors. The subtle use of color is apparent in furnishings, yet not too forcefully applied, allowing the interiors to maintain a purity of space and the natural feeling of the elements.

ABOVE: The living room is the gathering spot for the family. The pickled floors complement the interior walls and allow for sunlight to be absorbed. In keeping with Swedish interiors, Gretel and Libby chose not to install window treatments so that the flow of light from the exterior to the interior would continue without barriers. Indigenous elements from the property, such as the boulders for the fireplace, birch saplings for the ladder, and pine branches for greenery, also help to enhance the natural feel of the interior. An eighteenth-century Swedish chateau armoire anchors the room, a nineteenth-century American primitive tavern table adds a spot of color to an otherwise natural space, and the soft seating creates a comfortable area for the family to relax.

FACING, ABOVE: Shades of terra-cotta are expressed throughout the main living areas, grounded by the perfectly painted hutch; it took Libby and Gretel three attempts to achieve the desired color.

FACING, BELOW: The honey tone of the fruitwood table, the terra-cotta countertops, and the webbing of the bar stools all add warmth to the blonde interiors, creating balance and depth. Libby's added touches to the kitchen include installing a replica of a nineteenth-century Swedish plate rack. She and Gretel compromised on cabinets that were glass front as opposed to all open shelving.

ABOVE: A pair of nineteenth-century American painted finials
and an eighteenth-century Swedish pewter charger filled with
apples complement the eighteenth-century Swedish rococo
commode on which they are sitting. An early-nineteenth-century
Swedish chateau armoire is home to a wonderful collection of
antique quilts and linens.

FACING: Christopher and George's summer bedroom and
playroom.

While designing the kitchen's interior space, it took Libby and Gretel three attempts to achieve the right tone of terra-cotta for the dining room hutch. Using the hutch as a grounding color, they then added subtle hints of sage and terra-cotta throughout the rest of the kitchen and living room areas, creating a cohesive and balanced space.

Once the color schemes were chosen and there was a definitive plan, they began to select the right Swedish antiques to fill the spaces. Libby mixed some of her favorite pieces from her personal collection and shop inventory with comfortable and family-friendly furnishings to create a very simple yet sophisticated interior perfect for a family getaway with the feeling of a Swedish lake house in the archipelago.

Natural elements found on the property were also incorporated into the interior design. Another idea of George's was to use such indigenous materials as stone boulders for the thirty-foot fireplace, and the family gathered them over a three-day weekend. Chris fashioned white birch saplings (which are typically Swedish as well as New Hampshire's state tree) into ladders used to reach the windows in the cathedral-ceilinged great room. Gretel and Chris collected what they could use without disturbing the integrity of the landscape. The house is a true reflection of their love and respect for nature and their surroundings.

Simply put, when thinking of New Hampshire's state motto "Live free or die," it is clear that a natural, stress-free life is the objective. As crazy and harried as their daily lives get, it is comforting for these families to know that the lake house is just a few hours away. To quote Chris, "The lake house is a wonderful escape. It is not easy to get to, it is a lot of hard work to maintain, but it is so worth it!"

ABOVE: A European eagle flies with open wings over the window seat. On the front of it, Libby has drawn the family names and year of construction above Swedish motifs. A nineteenth-century French provincial chair is the perfect reading spot for lazy Sunday afternoons.

LEFT: Libby and George's bedroom reflects a Swedish sensibility by incorporating tonal, blonde wood hues and soft pale colors. In choosing a neutral floor covering—a Tabriz carpet—Libby was able to infuse color in a subtle yet powerful manner. The antique Swedish column clock and bed bench add to the elegant feel of the room. On a practical note, robin's-egg-blue Roman shades were added to the bedroom for those sleeping in the room who might be light sensitive.

FACING: A faux-marble-top nineteenth-century Swedish blue-painted commode works perfectly next to the natural blonde Adirondack four-poster bed. A subtle tone of terra-cotta seeps through the paint surface of the commode; the choice for placement of the piece was not without forethought. Balance and flow from space to space is essential for Libby in designing interiors.

FARMHOUSE ROMANCE

THE HOME OF EDIE BERNHARD VAN BREEMS

I've always had an attraction to buildings in romantic states of decay. Perhaps my predilection came from reading one too many issues of *World of Interiors* at a formative time in young adulthood. Under the editorship of Minn Hogg, the publication invariably featured neglected artists' garrets, Jacobean hunting lodges, and—this is what set my heart pounding—Swedish manor houses. I secretly yearned for an atmospheric wreck to restore and call my own.

FACING: The breakfast room table is a Swedish eighteenth-century double trestle table with a large center drawer. The dough bin on the table is carved from one large piece of wood and, as is common in these types of farm utensils, has an ancient repair made of steel. Wooden bowls were often bartered for other goods among farms. A single bowl can sometimes have as many as four to six initials of owners. The green-blue of the tall case clock and its carvings is typical of the Helsingland region of Sweden.

LEFT: A view of the house from under the birch tree and fieldstone wall.

ABOVE: The old Garland range came with the house and so, in keeping with the Swedish tradition of working with what you have, it was kept and moved into the new kitchen addition. Previous owners Steve and Katie Hylén had made the copper backsplash and hood. It is the perfect backdrop for a culinary copper collection that ranges from stamped royal crown copper pots to peasant ceremonial milk pails. The milk pail with leeks on the stove is an example of a decorative ceremonial milk pail. The pail would be delicately stamped with the bride and groom's initials, and the bride would then use this when gathering milk from the cows for special occasions. We can tell they are milking pails because of the tapered shape at the base, where a lady would hold the pail between her legs while milking a cow.

RIGHT: Russian silver and crystal ewers sit on an English cherry dining table ringed by Swedish Gustavian chairs. Prints by Crispin de Passe hang on either side of an early-nineteenth-century Swedish rustic blue armoire. A rare early-eighteenth-century baronial Swedish mirror displays a silver crest above its heavy black frame.

My first husband, Martin, unwittingly won my heart when he confessed that he wanted to fix up a derelict sculptor's studio in Westport. Set into terraced stone retaining walls, the miniscule building had been long ago abandoned to the raccoons. It was a marvelous project for us, and the restoration of the cottage was greatly satisfying. Several years later, with a two-year-old and another baby on the way, we went in search of a property on which to build a family home that would have more space. Rhonda Eleish and I had just opened Eleish van Breems Antiques, and we were both buying Swedish furniture not only for the store but for our own homes as well. I was looking forward to having a place to house my burgeoning collection of antiques. Flush from the success of the cottage restoration, Martin and I took on a historic 1760 property that had been half destroyed in a fire. The owner, ironically, was a Swede.

With two nature preserves, several gentleman farms, riding trails, and a golf course all within walking distance, the location seemed perfectly suited to raising two young boys. The area also had a revolutionary history: the British had camped in the property's fields on their 1777 march to Danbury. The literary history of the house is more recent; the writer and *New York Times* book review editor Anatole Broyard raised his family here for a time. During his ownership, he erected a writing shed in the back of the property that was eventually converted into a darkroom by the Swedish owners, Steve and Katie Hylén.

Having been a photographer, I found the darkroom appealing, but the most interesting thing I thought the Hyléns had done was to take this very American saltbox colonial and add Swedish details

FACING: End-of-summer hydrangeas push their heads up against the kitchen window. A small blue-painted trunk, initialed G.A.D., sits next to a baroque corner cupboard from Halsingland, Sweden. In the entrance hall, a Gustavian alder-root-veneered table holds a pewter platter filled with pears.

ABOVE: The large faience piece on the Swedish sideboard is a mystery. It was found in Sweden and appears to be eighteenth century. Rhonda and I speculate that it may have held brandied pears, honeyed apples, or cloudberry aquavit, but we may never know.

and paint colors. Because of the fire, very little of this remained when we started the restoration, but I was deeply inspired to also put a Swedish stamp on the interiors. Instead of painting the walls throughout the house as the Hyléns had done, I decided to have the walls rough plastered or brown coated with pigment added into the concrete for coloring. The color chosen was a pale yellow ochre mineral pigment seen on the outside of buildings throughout Stockholm's Gamla Stan—it changes color from beige to creamy sandstone, depending on the light. For other rooms, I chose not to add pigment but to let the concrete mixture dry to its natural pale pearl-gray color. Next to the original dark rough beams of the rooms, the walls looked authentically old and the Gustavian colors were the perfect background for a Swedish-themed interior. The chestnut floors, damaged by fire, were painstakingly hand-sanded and refinished while

other rooms were redone in new flooring that was pickled and scrubbed white. Most of the old rooms of the house face north and are very diminutive in scale. We decided that in order to enjoy the southern exposure with views to the stone walls and fields in the back of the property—as well as to have a relaxing family gathering place—we would build a large kitchen, den, and master bath onto the house.

An early-twentieth-century Swedish architect's table, based on an eighteenth-century design, is the focal point of the sitting room. The table displays various collectables of my sons, Lars and Martin, resident naturalists. A Gustavian armchair upholstered in blue-and-white ticking is placed in front of the table. On the wall hang two decorative mid-twentieth-century silhouettes by Borgese. The mirror over the fireplace is from 1810 and was made in Stockholm.

Swedish antique furniture, like most other continental antiques, can often feel a bit diminutive when placed in large newer homes. This furniture looks right at home in the 1820 sitting room due to the fact that the parlor's low-beamed ceilings and small footprint are similar to rooms found in Swedish country homes of the period. An early-nineteenth-century bench bed upholstered in beige check sits beneath a trio of Swedish mushroom prints.

A decade later, my affair with the house continues. I love how the light floods through the rows of cottage windows in the kitchen; the huge fireplace in the keeping room; and the built-in Swedish bed that my sons still love to roughhouse in. I enjoy using the house as a small laboratory, a place to try out new things, whether it is fabrics or paint finishes or even a recipe that we eventually introduce to our clients at the store. The most fun has been indulging in the Swedish copper collection, gardening, and my passion for all things Linnaean.

With fireplaces in almost every room and lots of small walls with windows, one great frustration has been a lack of wall space for bookshelves. A reader, I started out putting my books in closets, and they have now overflowed into artfully arranged piles, stacked on sides of sofas, lamely attempting to masquerade as side tables. This will not do much longer. The next project for the property just might be to find a site to build a barn studio with floor-to-ceiling bookshelves. I look out beyond the stone walls at the sight of the old root cellar, its entrance covered in layers of moss, vines growing up over its doors . . . I've got that old yearning.

FACING: A bedroom is an oasis, a place to dream, rest, and rejuvenate. Pictured here are some of my favorite things to ruminate on and relax with at the end of the day—a blue tall case Gustavian clock, a transitional Swedish gilt mirror, and a birch table of delicate lines by Stockholm cabinetmaker Jacob Stähl. The clock was a great find and works perfectly as something tall to stand next to the chimney in the master bedroom. The recessed panel on the Stähl table has a delicate brass banding and is perfect for placing flowers on.

ABOVE: The bedroom has too many windows. As a solution to not having a wall to place a bed against, Rhonda suggested that I place a corona over the bed to ground it. What a wonderful suggestion! With drapery, the bed feels enclosed and safe, and I can still awake and imagine being in a fairy bower. The historic documentary fabric hanging from the corona is called Ekkebyholm and is from Lars Sjoberg's now discontinued 1780 line for IKEA. I am an avid bibliophile, and the round pavilion table from the Eleish van Breems reproduction line holds all the books and magazines I need. Conveniently, the table has three leaves, and when I am entertaining large groups, this is brought downstairs and sets up easily next to the other table in the dining room.

ABOVE: A trunk from the far north of Sweden near Lapland is a prized possession. My great grandmother's family were Swedish reindeer ranchers from the Ångermanland region. Through the doorway can be seen a German armoire with a flower-and-urn decoration.

FACING: Sunlight pours into the upstairs reading nook lighting a nineteenth-century Swedish water bucket filled with a bouquet of late summer zinnias.

A SWEDISH-INSPIRED CABIN

THE CONNECTICUT HOME OF CAROLINE AND EDWARD WAGNER

*E*dward Wagner was very familiar with Litchfield County, Connecticut, having spent his childhood summers in Fairfield County, twenty-five miles to the south. In 1985, he and his wife, Carolyn, acquired the first of two parcels of land that make up their current property. Their plan was to have land with a sweeping view and extensive natural beauty. They were in no big rush, so Ed spent time poring over topography maps of northwest Connecticut, looking for the best view that would not, over time, be compromised by any obstruction. After Ed felt he had a good grasp of what areas he and Carolyn wanted to investigate, they contacted a realtor, and soon purchased their first seventy-acre parcel of hillside. It ascended from an elevation of 750 feet to 1,350 feet, over a distance of nearly a mile. It was a rugged climb that included a daunting rock face, but Ed's mother managed it at the age of eighty.

FACING: Located in the northern province of Dalarna, Sweden, are the copper and iron mines of Falun and Sala. Throughout the centuries, these mines have provided the local inhabitants a source of income and employment. The mines also provided the nation with copper and iron ore, used in pigment form, to create paint. With this in mind, the Wagners chose to stain their Swedish-inspired cabin Falun red, the red that is created when the copper ore is applied as a paint stain. Traditionally, Swedish farmhouses are stained with Falun red. Not only is the color vivid during the dreary winter months, it also maintains its color for a very long time, and therefore is a very practical form of protection for the house.

LEFT: Natural plantings, a view for miles, and plenty of sunlight make this home a little piece of heaven on earth.

The area was entirely wooded; Ed cut away enough growth to confirm that the view was extraordinary. According to Carolyn, "There was an enormous sense of gratitude when we first beheld the wide swath of farmland, distant hills, and a lovely lake to the southeast. Time seemed to stand still, and that view is a constant pleasure to us when we look out from our deck."

The Wagners desired a cottage that would be a counterpoint to their life in the city. They visited one built by local contractor Brian Wilson, and they loved the way he had constructed it. Mr. Wilson was the person they turned to when they were ready to build their own cottage in 1997.

The spirit of the house came from photographs of Swedish "stugas" and also from the summerhouses of family members the Wagners had visited in the Stockholm archipelago. The decision to stain the wooden cottage red was inspired by the special color of the farmhouses that dot the countryside throughout Sweden. Ed and his friend Gil Aimbez spent a lot of time trying to find the right red stain that would approximate that paint, and finally found one that closely resembled the famous Falun red. Named after the town of Falun, which has the largest copper mines in Sweden, Falun red uses copper ore as a pigment. The paint is very hardy; it has been used for centuries and is still applied summer after summer on Swedish cottages.

During construction, the question arose as to whether they wanted to add a guest room for visitors. The cottage is essentially one high-ceilinged great room with a sleeping loft. Once again, Ed drew upon his Swedish roots, and the couple decided that they would eventually build a small guesthouse on the property instead, as is common in Sweden. Twenty years earlier, during a hiking trip in northern Sweden, the Wagners stayed in a friend's tiny, remote cabin. The impressions

FACING, ABOVE: Mixing Swedish red-and-white cotton ticking fabric with Asian folk art adds a level of sophistication to the cottage. The lack of window treatments also allows for the maximum amount of sun the fill the space. Though diminutive in size, the cottage has all the creature comforts, including a discreetly hidden flat screen TV.

FACING, BELOW: A nineteenth-century Swedish trunk is used as a coffee table. Historically, the flat top chests were found commonly in the north of Sweden, while the dome top trunks were more commonly found in the south. Flat trunks were considered practical because of their stacking ability for storage, while dome-top trunks were considered a luxury due to the wasted space; hence, wealthier families had a larger percentage of dome-topped chests.

ABOVE: Collecting both American and Swedish folk art and displaying them together has been a passion for the Wagners and reminds them of their many trips to Sweden visiting Edward's family.

left by this experience remained with them, and in 2001, they read in the *New York Times* about an 8 X 10 foot Swedish Hermit's Cabin made of weathered pine board from old barns that could be ordered online from Sweden. They visited the website and contracted for the building to be installed on the property.

Prior to, and during, construction of their cottage, Ed and Carolyn began to think about what landscaping would work for their setting. According to Ed, the idea was to have "a cabin in the woods that is in harmony with the natural setting. We just wanted little fillings around the house that include native plants as much and as naturally as possible."

Since the completion of the cottage, the Wagners have been enjoying the privacy afforded by the quiet, secluded woodlands, and they look forward to the changes each season brings. Manhattanites for part of the week, they find their time at the cabin equally rewarding. Both love the natural beauty of native shadbushes, which are found in abundance all around the property, and they are eager to be there in late April to catch their brief blooming cycle. Summer foliage is lush and green, with birds attracted by the highbush blueberries that are mixed in with plantings of hayscented fern transplanted from large colonies elsewhere on the land. Fall brings the stunning leaf colors that the Litchfield Hills are known for, and winter affords theatrical shadows cast off from the barren trees onto the crisp, white snow. The joy of the woodland surroundings and one of the best views in Connecticut combine to make these among the most charming cabins ever built.

LEFT: Imported from Sweden, this summer cottage serves as a guesthouse for visiting friends and family. In 2001, the Wagners were thumbing through the *New York Times* and found the Thursday section on "small houses for sale." Intrigued by the idea of an antique Swedish "stuga" or house, the Wagners contacted the importing company in Sweden, and before they knew it, the Swedish designer, his carpenter, and the Wagners' contractor, Brian Wilson, were installing the small building on the property. Besides reassembling the stuga, the Wagners painted the window frames, reenforced the front door with new wood, added screens to the windows, added trim around the roof, and added a deck for their friend Bob, a frequent guest. Otherwise, the original patina of the house was kept weathered and untouched, maintaining its original integrity. The stuga has been lovingly nicknamed "The Bob Stuga."

FACING: The summer is a time in Sweden when families vacation together. This type of cottage dates back to the mid-nineteenth century and was built by workers, mostly from the cities, who were given small parcels of land (a form of a victory garden) by the Swedish government. This gift enabled even the less fortunate to be able to afford to escape from the city, have a garden, and enjoy the summer with their families.

LAGUNA LIGHT

THE BEACH HOUSE OF ANN AND TORBJÖRN MILLÄNG

My parents loved Laguna and this house. My father, Jack Cotter, was an environmental engineer who worked with the Laguna Conservation Trust in his free time and became very involved in the planning for what is now the protected beach walkway in front of the Montage Hotel. Both my parents had a great love for the unique landscape here in Laguna, and I remember they spent much of their time at the beach—swimming, surfing, walking, and watching the tides. When my brother, John, and I inherited the house, rather than sell it, we decided to keep it as a family retreat. To be back here has truly been like a spiritual homecoming." Though a native Californian, Ann Milläng had been living and raising her family in Sweden for the last twenty years. Thoughts of moving back home to Laguna had never been entertained, so the full nature of this return came as a surprise.

FACING: "We wanted to feel that we were at a Swedish beach house," says Ann Milläng. Nautical stripes and teak furniture from St. Barths' Belgian line bring the living room up to shipshape.

LEFT: When the second story was added to the house, it was decided that the stairwell would remain open to allow in as much natural light as possible.

Sweden has been central to Ann's life in many ways. As a student she studied architecture and design at the Swedish universities of Lund and Uppsala, followed by a Fulbright scholarship in urban planning. On the evening before catching the Trans-Siberian Railway to do post-graduate work in China, Ann made a fortunate decision to attend a black-tie event she'd been invited to in Stockholm. There she was introduced to Torbjörn Robert Milläng. It was, as they say, a coup de foudre, and the pair agreed to meet again in Australia. More than one meeting came of this plan and they were married not long after.

The couple established Swedish Blonde Collection in 1993, a company that sells Swedish furniture. "At first we were nervous about selling Swedish traditional furniture to the American market; we couldn't know how it would be received, but we found that it didn't matter if American clients were familiar with Swedish design. People would respond to something from their past that made them feel secure.

FACING: None of the furniture pictured is Swedish, but the grass rug, blue-and-white table linens, and linen-upholstered chairs are all reminiscent of those found in Swedish beach houses. They are also similar to the beach house interiors of the New England coastline.

ABOVE: Ann brought new life to a family heirloom by re-covering her Federal couch in a bright bold blue-and-white pattern by Ralph Lauren. Svenskt Tenn, the Swedish company known for its modern fabrics, uses bold patterns such as this to cheering effect. The blues and whites are soothing in the hot climate and are right at home by the beach.

ABOVE: The striped sofa bed was designed by Ann for her Swedish Blonde line and is built for American homes, using a standard twin-sized mattress.

LEFT: In the entrance foyer, a Swedish Gustavian sideboard stands sentry next to a Swedish console table from Ann's Swedish Blonde line. The round white mirror acts as a porthole reflecting the surrounding ocean. The planter is decorated with the Swedish royal crest, and nineteenth-century brass Swedish weights line up next to the Swedish brass candlesticks on the sideboard.

FACING: Terraced gardens, cascading down towards the sea, are found throughout the Laguna Hills landscape.

Perhaps it's because the Swedish aesthetic is similar to New England beach house interiors," considers Ann. "The furniture is simple and pared down with fresh fabrics and colors, and when they see this, clients respond from the heart and say 'This feels like home.' I also grew up with family on Cape Cod, and I know that this look is what I love too!"

Soon Swedish Blonde was being sold nationwide through catalog companies. Recently, Ann and Björn (as Torbjörn is known to all stateside) recently launched a new retail concept and web store called St. Barths Home, where the Swedish Blonde line can be found alongside other unique contemporary European furnishings and accessories. They are having fun furnishing the Laguna house with pieces from this collection.

Ann freely admits that when the moment arose to reclaim the family house in Laguna, it was a big transition from life on the Swedish archipelago for their children Jonathan and Julia, but that they now love and celebrate the differences. "This house is very different from my home in Sweden in that it is not very old," says Ann. "We still spend summers in the Swedish house, so I have had the advantage of living in both places."

Fortunately the family had a Swedish architect, Kurt Gorblich, to design the renovations. The exterior was inspired by Ann's family roots on Cape Cod and Nantucket. Kurt made it a point to design the space so light

could come in from as many angles as possible; he also opened up the stairway, a typically Swedish practice, to get more light to come down through the stairwell. A stunning all-white kitchen was designed by the Swedish company Kvänum Kök with special cross-pattern cabinets designed by Ann and Elizabeth, Kvänum Kök's owner. Pieces from the Swedish Blonde collection mix with Belgian furniture from St. Barths Home. Ann finds it interesting to infuse a Swedish mood without a lot of Swedish furniture. "What we are creating here in the beach house is all about a lightness and a sense of space," says Ann. "Striped and checked linens and cot-

ton textiles are key but most important is keeping the space open and light. It is a calm and serene style."

The Millängs use a famous quote from Carl Larsson in their company catalog that reads: "A home is not some lifeless object, but is alive and like all living things it must . . . change from moment to moment." And so the Laguna house is now in a vibrant renewal, transitioning from the last generation to the next, while its happy occupants stop often to watch the tides and remember.

FACING: Kitchen cabinets were designed in Sweden and brought over by container to fit out the Millängs' kitchen. White tiles reflect light and show food to advantage.

ABOVE: The terraced backyard serves as an extended outdoor living room. A deck creates another outdoor gathering area. Decks and outdoor pavilions are used throughout the summer months in Sweden as often as possible for gatherings and meals.

The bedroom was Swedish-inspired, especially the use of curtains around the plantation-style bed. Made of Swedish white linen, the window and bed curtains are so airy that they allow plenty of sunlight and ocean breezes to filter through while serving to soften the elements from the outside. Ann comments that "the Swedes did have canopy beds like this but generally they were painted white." The wall color is a typical Swedish blue beacon gray.

Window views looking out onto the Pacific Ocean allow Ann and Björn to pick up their spyglass to view Catalina Island in the distance. "It does remind me of a sea captain's desk," says Ann. Photos over the Korean chest are of her family on beach holiday in Cape Cod during the early 1900s; they add a sense of connection and place. A monkey's fist/ball sits on the Swedish commode.

Neoclassical Living in Atlanta

THE HOME OF ANGIE AND HUGH TYNER

A pair of majestic and verdant magnolia trees flanks the entrance to Angie and Hugh Tyner's Atlanta home. The stateliness of the trees, with their snow-white blossoms, is a precursor to the easy elegance to be found within what the Tyners modestly refer to as their "bungalow." The Tyners, who are antiques dealers specializing in Swedish eighteenth- and nineteenth-century pieces, knew that for this particular home they wanted to live with the best of their collection of Swedish Gustavian furniture. Gustavian furniture, Angie notes, possesses a coolness of the palette particularly soothing to come home to when living in the often-steamy humidity of Atlanta weather. The couple was also determined not to make the house too formal, and an ease of living was achieved by using linen for upholstery and curtains and sea grass carpeting throughout the home. What might have been horribly formal, when put together by the Tyners, becomes superb high country style, simultaneously inviting and whimsical.

FACING: Angie has brought the outside in by placing a Swedish plaster-cast garden statue of Pan on the stairwell landing. The custom-made plinth is painted faux gray marble. A pair of Swedish rococo armchairs covered in linen flanks the statue in perfect Swedish symmetry. The linen on the chairs ties in with the linen Roman shades above the windows. A sunshade can be pulled down from under the Roman shades, protecting the interiors from the harsh midday sun while still allowing one to look out.

LEFT: A late-Gustavian Swedish clock hangs in the stairwell; its glistening gilt ornament is echoed in an Italian mirror in the foyer.

The house is small and has a pleasant open layout with the living room, dining room, sunroom, and entrance hall all flowing smoothly into each other. Large bookcases stacked with volumes bound with vellum rich as country cream flank the French doors in the dining room. Collecting these rare vellum books is a passion the couple shares. Historically, vellum-bound books were so precious that they were kept in trunks for protection, and it was not until the late seventeenth century that Swedish book collectors began to display their books on actual shelves. Angie and Hugh decided to have custom bookshelves made for their library collection—all the better to admire the soft cream tones that match the carefully chosen eighteenth-century Gustavian décor of the living room and sunroom.

Swedish Gustavian furniture is based on French furniture influences from the court of Louis VI. King Gustav III and his coterie of designers and architects brought back the great-

est ideas from the French court, where interest in neoclassical form was enjoying a strong revival. Swedish Gustavian furniture is noted for its distilled purity of the French furniture forms, painted surfaces, and strong simple lines. Angie points out a masterfully carved pair of Swedish Gustavian chairs. Like everything else in the house, the chairs were selected under Angie's discerning eye for their elegant form and neutral paint color. Angie had all of the Swedish daybeds and settees reupholstered in soft linens with comfort in mind.

The overall feeling in the home is indeed Gustavian, yet the Tyners are not afraid to mix in pieces from other countries, which is typical of Swedish neoclassical decorating from around the time of the Enlightenment. After all, what would a room be without some artifacts from ancient classical cultures? The world has opened up significantly since Gustavian times, as evidenced by the many artifacts on display in the Tyners' living

room. A table covered in nineteenth-century South American *bultos* sits near a Gustavian glass-front secretary holding a collection of rare Swedish cameos and bronzes. The *bultos*, or freestanding wooden sculptures of Christ, the Virgin Mary, saints, and other holy figures, were used in churches and sanctuaries, and carried in religious processions; they make a dramatic display behind the living room settee. *Yua*, round disks used as currency from New Guinea, can be found mounted on Swedish side tables.

Not surprisingly, both Angie and Hugh are avid world travelers who met each other while on a Central American bird-watching expedition. As Hugh remembers it, the Resplendent Quetzal's metallic-glowing green plumage was what brought him on the trip, but once in Costa Rica, the only thing mesmerizing him was Angie's smile. Since that time, the couple has spent nearly every year traveling in New Guinea, Southeast Asia, and Brazil, from where they bring back furniture finds and accessories for their Atlanta shop. Located in the heart of Atlanta's Peachtree design district, A. Tyner Antiques has a premier collection of Swedish antiques mixed with

FACING: The custom-made chandelier hangs above a seventeenth-century Italian dining table topped by a wooden deer.

ABOVE: "Old volumes shake their vellum heads and tantalize just so . . ." —Emily Dickinson

a strong selection of Brazilian hardwood furniture, Indian carved architectural elements, and other exotic finds. The Swedish antiques, Angie and Hugh say, will always remain their first love. "The forms of the Swedish provincial furniture are so distilled and pure," points out Hugh, "that I never tire of collecting them. Each piece is almost modern sculpture." As for Angie, she says that she is most fond of the Swedish tall case clocks. "Admit it. You can't look at the Swedish clocks and not smile." ✳

FACING: Lion-headed eighteenth-century Swedish barrel chairs sit on either side of the Swedish neoclassical settee, also bearing carved lion heads. Lions were a symbol of royalty in Sweden. A collection of South American crowns sits on a Swedish blue baroque table.

ABOVE: A chimney floats in the middle of the house. What could have been a liability Angie makes a focal point by using the chimney sidewalls to display two Swedish tall case clocks. Shown here is a nineteenth-century Swedish tall case clock scraped down to its original soft sand colors. The fireplace mantels are topped by eighteenth-century French paneling.

ABOVE: A welcoming porch can be seen through the leaves of two magnolia trees.

FACING, ABOVE: The furniture is darker in the bedroom, where black Swedish side tables hold figural carved-wood lamps.

FACING, BELOW: A pair of Swedish mid-eighteenth-century chairs sits on either side of a massive baroque armoire. Carved with fruit and leaves, it is spacious enough to store an entire wardrobe.

The eighteenth-century chalk-blue Swedish table, with its
gently curving cabriole legs and hoofed feet, brings painted
texture into the bathroom.

Angie and Hugh have started putting large antique stone
garden planters into the courtyard garden.

SEASIDE: THE SWEDISH DREAM

THE BEACH HOUSE OF LISA AND BOB NESBITT

ふ

*I*n 1946, J. S. Smolian, entrepreneur and grandfather of Robert Davis (founder of the Seaside community), purchased eighty acres of land near Seagrove Beach, Florida. Thinking of making the plot of land a summer camp for his employees, Smolian put the idea before his business partner, who quickly dismissed such intentions. The land remained undeveloped; the project never begun. As the years moved on and the Smolian family continued to vacation on the shore, young Robert grew to love the area.

FACING: Here, a view of the house is seen from the dunes. One of the design challenges that presented itself when the house was being built was the obstructed views the dune presented. The solution was to locate the main living spaces on the second level, with the junior bedrooms on the ground level and the master suite above.

LEFT: Neoclassical elements incorporated into the exterior design give the house a timeless feel, while an unfinished timber (cedar) roof takes a Nordic approach. The use of one structural column instead of two was inspired by the works of Karl Friedrich Schinkel, Germany's greatest neoclassical architect, as well as by Swedish buildings dating from around 1890 that Gary Brewer, Partner-in-Charge on the project, had seen in Sweden while on an architectural tour. The placement of the column was chosen so that one could take advantage of the diagonal view of the coast.

Entranced by the land that his grandfather had loved and believed in, Robert Davis, now a developer, decided to pursue what his grandfather had started. With the help of Miami architects Andres Duany and Elizabeth Plater-Zyberk, Davis began to design a community based on the ideals of New Urbanism. According to the CNU (Congress for the New Urbanism), "New Urbanism is a growing movement that recognizes walkable, human-scaled neighborhoods as the building blocks of sustainable communities and regions. The Charter of the New Urbanism articulates the movement's principles and defines the essential qualities of urban places from the scale of the region to the individual building." Established in 1981 as the first town in the United States to embrace the theory of

New Urbanism, Seaside has become the template for generations to come.

During the design process for development, it became clear to the team that extensive research needed to be done. The decision was made to travel to the South, especially through coastal Florida, documenting and archiving ideas that would work well for the proposed community. According to the Seaside website, "Most of the buildings were studied in the context of small towns, and gradually the idea evolved that the small town was the appropriate model to use in thinking about laying out streets and squares and locating the various elements of the community."

When Lisa and Bob Nesbitt decided that it was time to

FACING: Neutral interiors and unstructured window treatments are in keeping with Swedish design and interiors. A decorative neoclassical wall mural is reminiscent of the attractive interior decorations of Gustavian Sweden. A pair of Swedish klismos chairs flanks the fireplace, adding to the Gustavian mood of the room. French doors that surround the room are actually pocket doors enabling the space to completely open up, extending to the living porch. According to Lisa, "The Scandinavian feel of the home is from Robert and Gary's vision. When they suggested that direction to us, we agreed immediately. I've always been drawn to images I've seen of homes decorated with a Scandinavian feel."

ABOVE: The neutral, tonal color palette and natural flooring create a spacious feel in a smaller space. The interior space is at ease with the exterior space; a sense of balance is achieved.

LEFT: Neoclassical detailing and trompe l'oeil add sophistication to the Nesbitt's Seaside home. According to Stern, "The house is like a big cabinet. Every surface is accounted for."

build their dream vacation home after living in two other Seaside properties, they called upon Robert A. M. Stern Architects for help. Inspired by a shingle-style house that Stern had designed on the East Coast, as well as other of his works, Bob enlisted the help of the firm. Although a smaller project than what the firm is usually commissioned for, Robert A. M. Stern, also dean of the Yale School of Architecture, had always held a soft spot for the Seaside community and therefore decided to take on the project. According to Stern, "It's a great example and model, and it has been emulated all over the world. It is not only pedestrian-friendly, but also kid-friendly. There's a real intimacy to it. So many other developments have copied it that it has transformed the panhandle of Florida."

Inspired by this project, Gary Brewer, a partner at RAMSA as well as Partner-In-Charge on the Nesbitt house, referred back the countless photos he had taken while on an architectural tour of Sweden (sponsored by the

FACING: The master bedroom opens onto its own terrace, extending the interior space to the outdoors. A nineteenth-century Swedish Gustavian bench sits at the foot of the bed, while simple window treatments add an elegant touch.

ABOVE: The master bath feels naturally connected to the outside elements. Every surface, every detail was done with tremendous thought and planning. The bathroom cabinets refer back to Gustavian Sweden by applying the classical Gustavian diamond motif to the doors, and an antique French Lalique chandelier reflects nature with a sparrow and her nest filled with eggs.

Swedish *potskaps* sit on either side of a guest bedroom bed
and are the perfect night tables for areas limited in space. The
form was originally used as a cabinet to house the potty cup
in Gustavian Sweden; however, with modern plumbing, it has
become a wonderful form for a bedside table.

Institute of Classical Architecture) a few months back. While it was still fresh in his mind, Gary was amazed at how the Gustavian structures he had seen were visually high style, but in actuality, the bones were wooden structures. He loved the beautiful character of the Swedish homes, and because of that, he wanted to create the American version of Swedish design in the Nesbitt home. This would be in keeping with the strict Seaside construction guidelines requiring buildings to be constructed from timber. And the cool, soft interior colors and furnishings of the Swedish Gustavian era were perfect for a home by the sea.

According to Lisa, "You can visit Seaside for an enjoyable day; but to truly experience it, you need to stay for several days. Seaside itself fosters a connection to life in a way that is often difficult to achieve in our daily lives back at home. The pace is slow, and

Nautical blues and whites not only fall into the range of a Swedish color palette but also reflect the close proximity of the home to the shore. A Swedish Gustavian chair and writing desk are visible through the threshold into the guest bedroom.

the town layout invites you to walk, bike, visit, relax, and connect with people you have in your home and people in homes around you. For adults, this community is so vibrant. There are wonderful art galleries, shops, and great restaurants within walking distance. For families, there are weekly movies on the main lawn, a repertory theater, and, of course, the beach. For a brief period, while we were building this house, we owned a unit in a gated condominium complex about five miles from

Seaside. Our son was about ten at the time. After going to the beach, the pool, and riding his bike in the parking lot of the condominium complex, he said, 'Mom, I want to go back to Seaside. I miss my town. I'm not a condo man.' Moral of the story: even ten-year-old boys understand New Urbanism at the root level."

To quote the Seaside website, "Learn to feel small again."

FACING: The living porch, with its beautiful views, makes outdoor living easy. In Sweden, the summer months are cherished and nature is respected. The spirit of Sweden and those summer months are captured on this terrace. Gary Brewer, when designing the home, was very sensitive to this, given his knowledge of the Nesbitts' love of the outdoors as well as a keen understanding of the Swedish love of nature from his wife, who is Swedish.

ABOVE: No small wonder that Seaside was chosen as the location for the 1998 movie *The Truman Show*, staring Jim Carrey and Laura Linney. A pristine shore, architecture that is complementary to its surroundings, and the sense that there is complete harmony within the community all acted as the perfect setting for the film.

WOODSTOCKHOLM: THE ARTIST COTTAGE

THE WEEKEND ESCAPE OF HEIDI AND DAVID FREILICH

*B*uilt in 1902 as an artist's studio and located across the Mill Brook from the Historic Woodstock Inn, David and Heidi Freilich's weekend cottage is not only a charming escape but also an ode to David's aspirations as an artist. The restoration of the cottage, which took two and a half years, was David's opportunity to take a blank canvas and compose from inspirations he had collected from his many years of travel and research. As a result, each color, architectural element, and interior furnishing was well thought out and composed to create a completely balanced and cohesive design.

FACING: The dramatic window is original to the building and is typical of the period and style of artist cottages in Woodstock (many built by Hervey White for visiting friends). David loves the reflective light it allows in the house.

LEFT: Woodstock's Mill Stream Bridge is within an arm's reach of the Freilich's cottage, as is the famous Woodstock Inn, where guests have included Bob Dylan, Arlo Gutherie, and the Rolling Stones.

ABOVE: Built in 1902, Woodstockholm took two and a half years to restore, and is now the Swedish-inspired summer cottage of the Freilich family.

LEFT: David designed this window, incorporating a rural Swedish cornice/frieze on the top, with a heart design taken from a window found at "Peterhof," or *Petrodvorets* ("The Russian Versaille"), the czar's summer palace in St. Petersburg, Russia.

FACING: An early-twentieth-century Canadian rabbit hook rug hangs over a nineteenth-century Swedish Karl Johan–style table, and a Swedish blue-painted child's rocking horse rests on a nineteenth-century Amish rag carpet. Flanking the table is a pair of early nineteenth-century American country ladder-back chairs that were found on one of the Freilich's many antiquing adventures.

The Freilich family discovered Woodstock, in the historic Hudson Valley of New York (whose red barns, stone fences, and horse farms echo the landscape features of Sweden), many years before acquiring their cottage. Their love of the local art scene and nature eventually prompted them to look for a weekend getaway for their family, and by luck, they stumbled upon the cottage.

Before 1902, Woodstock was a small farming and trade village, with some industry that was, on occasion, visited by artists looking for compelling Catskills vistas for their landscape paintings. In 1902, Ralph Radcliffe Whitehead, a wealthy British expatriate, created Woodstock's first artist colony, Byrdcliffe.

Along with kindred spirits Hervey White and Bolton Brown, Whitehead built a community in the spirit of John Ruskin and William Morris' British Arts and Crafts movement.

Woodstock today remains a vibrant artists' colony. Almost ninety years since its founding, the Woodstock Artists Association Gallery still remains in its original building on Tinker Street.

Professionally, David has worked for most of his career as in-house counsel for a Swedish company. He and his wife, Heidi, a legal nurse consultant, share an enthusiasm for traditional and contemporary Swedish design and aesthetics. According to David, "most of my Swedish friends have access to

ABOVE: A Swedish early-nineteenth-century reproduction print of
a swan hangs above a nineteenth-century American original-paint
drop-leaf table.

FACING: An early-eighteenth-century Irish tea table is placed next
to a nineteenth-century American ladder-back chair and yellow
dry goods barrel. A late-nineteenth-century Swedish tole-painted
shoemaker's sign hangs above the table.

ABOVE: A nice contrast to the structured Adirondack chairs, soft seating is introduced into the living space to add a bit of comfort and function. Additionally, a pair of nineteenth-century Swedish farm chairs from Jämtland adds to the eclectic nature of the room.

FACING: David found this nineteenth-century Swedish Mora tall case clock in the Marché aux Puces (the flea market) in Paris. What attracted him to the clock were the patina and the painted surface, which had been scraped down to the original blue-and-sienna base.

a weekend cottage or summer home. These getaways are a mainstay of their culture, which I have long admired. I've been privileged to visit many such homes over the years. We finally decided to follow the example of our friends and re-create our own 'slice of Sweden' when this property came into our lives." Located in the center of Woodstock, David and Heidi's cottage is aptly named Woodstockholm.

Nearness to water, nature, and serenity are a few of the things that come to mind when one thinks of the ideal location for a Swedish summer refuge, where modern-day urban pressures are quickly shed. According to David, "we fell in love with Woodstockholm the moment we saw her. For us, the lines of the house and symmetry echoed the Palladian villas that were built from the mid-seventeenth century and on in Sweden— of course, on a much smaller scale in our example. The location was also perfect, situated alongside a soft-spoken brook with a swimming hole, across from a small bridge, and surrounded by towering pines." As a bonus, it's only a short stroll to the thriving arts village of Woodstock, where galleries, music, and eateries can be enjoyed year-round.

It took about two years of weekend carpentry and cultivation to transform this classic Woodstock bunga-low into a typified Swedish summer cottage. Several of the couple's close friends enthusiastically pitched in. Left intact was the original exterior frame that has a simple and timeless design. The peaked roof with gabled ends and a soaring studio window give the cottage a big spirit. It readily absorbed a new crimson roof and coat of clas-sic yellow-ochre paint, both of which are traditional to Swedish summer homesteads. The frontal prospect is further defined by a pair of arching Victorian leaf fronds that were suggested by their friend, noted Americana dealer Stephen Score of Boston. These airy elements

help to strike the balance between rusticity and refinement that was sought by Woodstockholm's owners.

Inside the cottage, David painted most of the walls with rural and neoclassical designs that enhance visual appeal and historic interest. Color inspiration for the living room walls, for example, was found at Groddegården, a homestead in the North of Gotland, Sweden. Blue tones were infused into the room by way of antique barn boards found in Goshen, New York, and a pale white was added for its soothing effects and color value. The living room is charming and sophisticated yet rustic, capturing the true spirit of an authentic Swedish summer cottage.

"We painted the living room floor and the old brick fireplace in order to reflect incoming light from the opposite picture window. Luckily, we stumbled on some antique barn boards with an untouched, beautiful sea-blue surface. Installed around the fireplace, they work with the floors to provide a pleasing backdrop for the room's furnishings," says David.

The creative spirit continued when designing the kitchen and bedroom spaces. Being both visual and resourceful (both very Swedish traits), David and Heidi cleverly reversed the remaining antique barn boards they found in Goshen, sanded them, and installed the wide planks as kitchen and hall flooring.

Blue, David's favorite color, continues as a signature shade throughout the house. The kitchen, Heidi's favorite room and her creative arena, is kept fresh and spacious with butter-toned walls while splashes of blue are added to accessorize. The master bedroom reflects an understated elegance highlighted by classical blue-toned wall murals that were inspired by examples taken from manor

ABOVE: A collection of Scandinavian nineteenth-century treen and tole wear is displayed to give the kitchen a punch of color.

FACING: Early-twentieth-century American Adirondack cottage chairs (circa 1930) with their original pink-painted surfaces mix well with a nineteenth-century Swedish faux-marble-painted trunk from Dalarna, Sweden. Above the fireplace mantel hangs a nineteenth-century over-mantel painting from Upstate New York or perhaps New Hampshire.

ABOVE: Represented by the James Cox Gallery in Woodstock, New York, contemporary Swedish artist Clem Hallquist is a Woodstock resident artist of Swedish American stock. Featured on the loft wall is a fine example of his stunning work.

FACING: The kitchen is where Heidi's creative energies are focused when in Woodstockholm. Given that the kitchen is spacious and light, Heidi finds inspiration by just being in the room.

houses the couple has explored. The artist's bedroom is as an artist's bedroom should be—flowing with color and inspirations—and the loft bedroom is wonderfully nautical with marine-blue and sky-white tones and a sunny mood.

According to David, "We like to mix common things with a few precious objects, the everyday with the special, clutter and inspiration. Atmosphere is important to us."

Woodstockholm is truly a bit of "Sweden outside of Sweden," a special place where there is no TV or Internet, just the sound of music in the background and the spirit of creative and inspired energy.

FACING: David's interest in decorative painted surfaces led him to take a class years ago with Rubens Teles, from the faculty of the Folk Art Institute in New York City. Mr. Teles was instrumental in establishing the movement to help preserve original paint finishes in the United States. Beginning with decorative surfaces on furniture, it took David years to perfect the paint techniques he used for the interior of the cottage.

The faux wood grain painted effects of the dado were modeled after the painted paneling found in one of the large conference rooms at Drottingholm Palace, originally the queen's summer palace and currently the private residence of the Swedish royal family.

ABOVE: Among the artists lured to Woodstock by the newly established artist colony were two talented Swedes, John F. Carlson and Carl Eric Lindin. Both Carlson and Lindin were landscape painters who were passionately captivated by the fields, hills, and rivers backed by the distant rolling waves of Woodstock's surrounding mountains. Both men went on to become instrumental founders of the Woodstock Artists Association, and Lindin in particular became a champion for encouraging all artists in their pursuits, whether modern or traditional. Lindin viewed the association as "a place where all the creeds could meet and where the divine idea of beauty could be seen and perhaps understood, in its many differentiations." (see www.jamescoxgallery.com)

The above portrait of a young woman by Carl Eric Lindin is courtesy of Clem Hallquist through the James Cox Gallery, Woodstock, New York.

LEFT: According to the Ask Art website, "Carl Lindin (1869–1942) left his homeland of Sweden in 1887 for the United States. He settled in Chicago, Illinois, and studied at the Chicago Art Institute. In 1893, Lindin traveled to France to study painting. During the four years he spent in Paris, the young artist studied under Benjamin Constant and Jean-Paul Laurens at the Académie Julien and with Aman-Jean. Lindin returned to Chicago in 1897. While in Chicago, Lindin became close friends with Hervey White, a writer and poet who was instrumental in establishing Woodstock as an artist haven.

The above portrait of a young woman by Carl Eric Lindin is courtesy of Clem Hallquist.

DAISYFIELDS: SWEDISH SPLENDOR

THE CONNECTICUT HOME OF CYNTHIA AND BRUCE BABER

Built in 1927 by the owners of an adjacent historic property, the original charming brick cottage in Weston, Connecticut, was intended as a wedding gift for their son and his new bride. Journalist and author Amy Vanderbilt and her husband, photographer Hans Knopf, purchased the home in 1945, and they and their three sons enjoyed the property as a summer home for many years. Mrs. Vanderbilt named the property Daisyfields, and she referred to it fondly in her writings. The home is the current residence of Cynthia Gates Baber (whose mother is Norwegian) her husband, Bruce, and their two children.

FACING: The family room, which flows off the kitchen, is a comfortable resting spot for the family and a place for casual dinners. The colors chosen for the soft seating are bolder than in most of the house in order to reflect the color tones of the Swedish tall case allmoge clock.

LEFT: Built in 1927, Daisyfields was originally a cottage for neighboring newlyweds. The brick section of the house is the original cottage.

During her tenure in the home, Mrs. Vanderbilt purchased a vintage dairy barn that was in the process of being dismantled in nearby Westport, and had it moved, beam by beam, to Daisyfields. The barn served as her writing studio for many years. In the upstairs of the barn, she researched and wrote her most famous work, *Amy Vanderbilt's Complete Book of Etiquette*, which was published in 1952. *Amy Vanderbilt's Complete Cookbook*, published in 1961, was also written at Daisyfields. In her cookbook, Mrs. Vanderbilt describes in detail the kitchen in the main house at Daisyfields, where she tested recipes for her book and entertained friends and family. She reported that "one wall is solid with cookbooks," a feature that Cynthia, an avid cook, has repeated with numerous Scandinavian titles included in her extensive cookbook collection. Mrs. Vanderbilt discussed and provided resources in her cookbook for the preparation of a traditional Swedish smorgasbord, which she learned of firsthand in Stockholm with her sons. Andy Warhol,

ABOVE: The formal entrance to the Babers' home was part of the addition connecting the original cottage to the new wing that was commissioned by the Vanderbilt-Knopf family in 1958.

FACING: A Swedish reproduction Gripsholm bench provides the perfect grounding balance to the colorful contemporary still-life oil painting above. A classic Swedish muted plaid fabric was used on the traditional plump feather cushion of the bench. Inspired by the subtle application of a cream color found in the still life that graces the foyer wall, the foyer color (Farrow and Ball Cream #44) helps create a calming and inviting entry. The Babers' extensive art collection includes pieces by several Scandinavian artists.

one of Mrs. Vanderbilt's many artist friends, illustrated her cookbook.

During the Vanderbilt era, the charming potting shed on the property served as a bunkhouse for the children, complete with a wood-burning stove. Typically with many Swedish summer country properties, outbuildings on family compounds and farms were frequently used as guesthouses for visiting family and friends. The potting shed reminded Cynthia of those small houses, and was one of the many things about the property that was reminiscent of summers of her youth spent in Scandinavia with family. Cynthia's ancestral family farm in Norway, named Eskeland, had similar outbuildings.

In 1958, the Vanderbilt-Knopf family added a kitchen wing (which included two upstairs bedrooms and a bath) to the house and more than doubled the size of the cottage. In 1961, the art director of *Sports Illustrated Magazine* and his fashion designer wife purchased the property, where they resided with their children for nearly forty years. A separate garage was added by a later owner, increasing the number of buildings on the property to four.

In 2006, Cynthia and Bruce Baber acquired Daisyfields as their family home. The couple was particularly taken with the natural beauty of the four-acre property and the adjoining five-acre wildflower preserve. As with most historic properties, major electrical, plumbing, and heating issues had to be addressed. The various systems updates became part of an overall renovation of the kitchen, which Cynthia wanted to reflect her Scandinavian roots and culture. Her choices of rustic faux-painted custom cabinetry, a Nordic color palette, and the use of a natural-wood island countertop accomplished that feel. The kitchen is an elegant reflection of Scandinavian design—clean, simple, functional, and very current.

Once the kitchen was completed, Cynthia and her design consultants from Eleish van Breems Interiors then addressed the interior colors of each room to complement her Swedish antiques. Creams and whites became the backdrop for the living room and upstairs bedrooms, while such warmer colors as terra-cotta and Falun red became essential in the dining room and the combined kitchen and family room.

Peppered throughout the house are mixes of Swedish and French antiques that blend seamlessly together. The transition to a Swedish country interior had been Cynthia's goal for many years, so the process of "weeding out" the old and bringing in the "freshness" has been an ongoing process and has yielded a timeless look.

In the living room space, neutral and tonal creams replaced the former color palette. By mixing several Swedish Gustavian antiques and handcrafted reproductions with the Babers' existing French Provençal antiques, a very sophisticated mood was created for the room. The creamy color chosen for the walls reflects light into the room,

With their children now grown, the Babers felt that it was time to introduce more creams and neutrals into the living spaces. The decision was made to tackle the living room first by applying Farrow and Ball Cream #44 to the walls, thereby creating a soft and light-absorbing color that is naturally Swedish. In keeping with an ode to Carl Linnaeus, the famous Swedish naturalist, the fabric choice for the two slipper chairs was inspired by the botanicals of Linnaeus. Complementary neutrals followed on the remaining upholstered soft seating, incorporating a range of tonal linens from Rogers and Goffigon.

A Swedish reproduction demi-lune is the perfect side table for the narrow space between the silk, unstructured window treatments. As with the dining room, a glass-top table appears in the living room. Sweden is world renowned for hand-blown glass, and the application of glass in many different forms as accents provides an additional element of interpretation with Scandinavian roots.

A nineteenth-century Swedish Gustavian-style buffet greets guests as they enter the living room from the dining room.

and furnishings in natural linens and homespun fabrics add to the overall feel. Window treatments were kept simple and minimal to allow light in and to invite in the natural beauty of the property through the numerous windows.

The dining room presented a color challenge: How to establish a warm, inviting atmosphere without reducing the sense of space in the room? After considering several stronger colors, the team finally found the right color of terra-cotta, which is used on many of the historic buildings in Stockholm. The choice reflected another return to Cynthia's roots and a color that reflects a Scandinavian sensibility.

The kitchen, the true heart and soul of the house, balances out tonal neutrals as well as incorporates Falun red. Falun red, a historic Swedish pigment stain that contains copper ore for color and is still used today, was chosen as the color applied to the center island. A wonderful collection of antique Swedish copper is displayed and supported by the Falun red hues of the center island. Stainless steel was introduced to complement the taupes, grays, and neutrals of the natural-honed granite countertops. The kitchen cabinets and trim were faux painted in a rustic mottled gray by Eugenia Davis, an artist friend of the Babers from Atlanta, Georgia.

Cynthia's objective for the master bedroom was to establish a room that could serve as a comfortable private retreat. Tonal whites and crisp linens present a fresh space that is soothing and pleasing to the eye. The core value of the space is Scandinavian—bright, sunny, simple, and elegant.

An eighteenth-century Swedish tall case clock stands proud in the Babers' dining room. The room features French Provençal chairs and a nineteenth-century walnut buffet showcasing inherited family silver, which complements the wrought-iron, glass-top dining table that mixes French country with a Scandinavian twist. Unstructured window treatments soften the walls of windows while allowing in natural light. A warm terra-cotta wall color (Farrow and Ball Loggia #232), inspired by the historic buildings of Gamla Stan—otherwise known as Old Town in Stockholm—graces the walls. The country bead board ceiling was painted a soft complementary pale taupe to create the appearance of height. Antique hand-hewn beams were added to the dining room ceiling and walls to complete the authentic Scandinavian feel of the room.

Cynthia's passion for the culinary arts translates not only into creating healthy and organic meals for her family but also into collecting a variety of Swedish antique culinary copper and wooden farm ware.

Included in the extensive nineteenth-century Swedish copper collection shown in this photo are a small copper milk pail, beautifully displayed with wildflowers, and a copper vodka flask of the type used by nineteenth-century travelers, workers, and soldiers.

Cynthia fell in love with the artisan Dala horse, a contemporary version of the traditional Dala horse, while visiting a local Swedish antiques shop. Inspired, Cynthia and her team commissioned muralists and decorative painters Ester Den Breems and Katie Maki to paint the inset panel next to the horse as a complement to its tones. An avid reader and book collector, Cynthia relied on her extensive collection of Scandinavian design books as a reference source, finding the perfect simple decorative motif to be reproduced in her kitchen.

LEFT: A Scandinavian by heritage, Cynthia's love of Swedish interiors and antiques has been lifelong.

ABOVE: Color inspiration for the kitchen came from the Babers' nineteenth-century Swedish tall case clock. Typical of the allmoge clocks from Dalarna, Sweden, this clock's color palette consists of Falun red and tonal blue, gray, and taupe.

FACING: The focus on decorative detail extends to the smallest spaces. Bothered that the gap above the kitchen sink window was too bare, Cynthia commissioned decorative painter Ester Den Breems and her team to paint a simple yet elegant Swedish motif that would be in concert with the wood panel across the room that they had just painted. Notice that the tone in color is once again derived from the same color values as the Falun red.

With Norwegian roots, crisp, pressed white linens are a must. Cynthia wanted the master bedroom to be a refuge. By keeping it simple, clean, and tonal, she has achieved a space that is not only soothing but also calming. Swedish reproduction commodes flank both sides of the bed. The Swedish headboard, upholstered in pale blue linen, is a handcrafted reproduction. The botanical ceramic Tiffany lamps add a touch of nature to the room. Soft, subtle blue-and-cream lattice carpeting grounds the space without detracting the eye from the crisp essence of the room.

The fieldstone kitchen terrace, with its ivy-covered walls and surrounding stone benches, is a natural gathering place for entertaining family and friends. Perennial, fern, and culinary herb gardens surround the area.

ABOVE: Inside the much-loved potting shed is a collection of English and Swedish antique garden elements and tools that continue to be used in the garden. Nineteenth-century English tin and copper watering cans are used to water the perennial and herb gardens. A nineteenth-century English terra-cotta rhubarb forcer stands ready for use. A nineteenth-century Swedish painted pine berry-washer still serves to wash wild summer berries gathered on the property. Colorful Marimekko gardening aprons hang from a rustic antique Swedish rack.

RIGHT: The window box of the potting shed garden is over-stuffed with fragrant culinary herbs used daily for family meals.

FACING: The potting shed and Amy Vanderbilt's writing barn.

THE SWEDISH POOL PAVILION

DESIGNED BY RICHARD HERSHNER

When interior designer Richard Hershner was brought in by a client to design the interiors of a family retreat in Connecticut, he was anticipating doing a timeless American adaptation of a period Connecticut River Valley house. Historic homes are strung like pearls along the winding old byways of this wooded section of the Nutmeg State, and, although the client's property was new, they wanted a home that would appear to have been there since Revolutionary times. Hershner, known for the historical integrity of his interiors as well as for his sensitivity to the demands of modern life, was clearly the man for the job. A fruitful design partnership emerged between client and designer, and several years after the completion of the main house interiors, Hershner was called in once again to design what was to become known as the Swedish Pool Pavilion.

FACING: The pool house is situated behind the main house and the barn, and is a relaxing destination just a short stroll down a hill from the historically inspired garden, also designed by Hershner.

LEFT: The terrace of the pool house is situated tantalizingly close to the water's edge. The pool beckons.

The homeowner, a busy mother of four, realized that the family needed a place to gather away from the main house. "We wanted a destination on a nice day as I felt we were inside too much. The idea of a pool pavilion as an indoor-outdoor retreat, which was suggested by Richard's friend and fellow designer Bruce Budd, appealed to me from my experience in the Caribbean." The challenge to Hershner was to create an outbuilding by the pool that would be true to the New England setting and the historic nature of the house. He decided to tap into the Federal taste as it is the next phase in the development of American building style after the Colonial period. His idea to use a vaulted ceiling in what would become the Federal-inspired pool house was rooted in the gathering halls of the late eighteenth and early nineteenth centuries, where meetings and dances were held. The surprise when entering the building is that you are transported into a pure Swedish interior.

"Richard really listened to me," states the client. "I've always loved Swedish-painted furniture. I love the palette, how scrubbed, how fresh everything looks—and so uncluttered. We really inspired each other, and it was very exciting knowing that this building was going to be so unique and different!" Richard notes, "There is a certain honesty to vernacular Federal buildings

ABOVE: A ship's model sits on top of a Swedish early-nineteenth-century yellow ochre buffet with fluted diamond panels.

FACING: A twentieth-century Gripsholm Swedish chair upholstered in a light-blue washed linen provides comfort in the sitting area. A rustic New Hampshire chair with rush seat balances the more formal aspect of the rococo sofa to create a convivial sitting area on the western end of the room.

ABOVE: A large chandelier of hand-cut tin oak branches hangs over the early-nineteenth-century Swedish drop-leaf table. A set of six Leksand Swedish chairs are pulled around the table for casual yet elegant summer dining.

FACING: Through the kitchen window, above the soapstone sink, one can observe the comings and goings of the barn and the main house—an advantage when on the lookout for your dinner guests! The storage shelves are left open, as would have been the case in a period buttery. A collection of blue feather-edge pearl ware dates from the 1850s. Early fall heirloom apples from the orchard sit in a nineteenth-century wooden bowl.

in this country, with their pared-down, almost sparse, interiors. The aesthetic is similar in Swedish Gustavian interiors, so the concept of having a pool pavilion done in Swedish style was actually a fairly natural progression. Both periods have their roots in neoclassicism."

Set down a hillside behind the garden and barn, the pavilion has three sets of tall French doors. The doors open inward, as recommended by Bruce Budd. The easy transition from indoor to outdoor is dramatic, as large wooden outer doors, also advised by Budd, are rolled open to reveal the view of a pergola with cascading white clematis. The pool, located just steps

beyond the threshold of the doorways, was modeled to have its interior surface appear as a natural pond.

At the center of the pavilion's spacious interior main room sits a robust early-nineteenth-century Swedish gateleg table and above it a chandelier of tin-cut oak leaves hangs from a barrel-vaulted ceiling. A Swedish rococo sofa from the Lars Sjöberg Museum Collection, along with a comfortable Gripsholm-style armchair and a rustic New Hampshire chair, creates a convivial sitting area on the western end of the room. Directly opposite, on the eastern end of the room, is a fully functional kitchen primed for all manner of culinary considerations. A traditional Swedish

feeling was achieved using historical mineral pigment paints of gray and a deep marigold hue. The flooring is antique French limestone pavers in various sizes. Functionality rules in the back three rooms where built-in shelves and benches neatly hold all manner of appropriate sunning and swimming gear, and his-and-her changing rooms on either side of the bathroom open onto an outdoor shower. The simplicity of the rooms is in keeping with a minimalism associated with traditional Swedish summerhouses, where the focus is on nature and the nearby woods. Make no mistake; although the mood in the structure is relaxed, everything down to the hardware detailing and textiles are all of the finest quality. "A premise for me in designing a home for a family is that I want it to be friendly and casual in feeling. Yet, you want something that people can grow into over time. It is important to use quality furniture and materials that age gracefully with wear. In this venue, I let them use everything," says Richard.

"It's exciting the day the pool house opens," says its satisfied owner. "From that moment onward—breakfast, lunch, and dinner—you can find us down there. I love the direction this building took; its functionality and visual grace have definitely enhanced our enjoyment of the property. Richard is right. There is just something very honest about it."

ABOVE: A simple changing room with hooks and benches for clothing and towels opens onto an outdoor shower. A nineteenth-century tin oil lantern converted to electric makes an elegant hanging light. Curtains in the changing rooms are of blue-and-white hand-loomed fabric.

FACING: Here is the pool house pergola, awash in a sea of white-flowering fall clematis.

WHITE WISTERIA

THE HOME OF SHANNON AND ANDREW NEWSOM

*A*s a young foreign exchange student, Shannon Newsom found herself at age eighteen in Hamina, Finland, some twenty to thirty miles west of the Russian border. A native of Texas, she had been invited to her host family's summer stuga, or cottage, and, to her pleasure, came to experience the ritual of sauna, wild berries, and the long, lingering days of the midnight sun. Ten years after that idyllic introduction to Scandinavian life, Shannon was living in Appalachia and there encountered the similarities between Shaker furniture and Finnish country antiques of the stuga she had visited all those years ago. Finnish eighteenth-century antiques, it must be noted, bear all the hallmarks of their Swedish cousins as Finland was a part of Sweden until 1801. "I was surprised that Shaker furniture reminded me of Swedish and Finnish antiques so much in its functionality and elegant lines," muses Shannon. "It really brought back to me my attraction to Swedish furniture design."

FACING: A delicate French bistro table makes the perfect place for casual breakfast dining in the Newsom's kitchen.

LEFT: The face of a Swedish blue-painted clock secretary. Swedish nineteenth-century clockworks were often made by manufacturers other than the cabinetmaker who made the clock case. The main works manufacturers were located in Mora, Sweden, and cabinetmakers from all over Sweden would order their clock mechanism from there; hence, the ubiquity of "Mora clocks."

ABOVE: A pitcher of spring peach blossoms sits on an early-
nineteenth-century Swedish clock secretary in the living room.
An eighteenth-century hand-carved bracket and urn on the wall
are from France.

FACING: A pair of rare Gustavian chairs sits on either side of an
eighteenth-century Swedish console table in the living room. The
table is topped by a classical plaster sculpture of a young boy.

ABOVE: An eighteenth-century sofa from northern Sweden adorned with pillows of antique linen makes the perfect place in the library to curl up with a book. An early-nineteenth-century Swedish toy horse sits under a Swedish nineteenth-century baroque table with barley twist legs.

FACING: Eighteenth-century blue books sit under an Italian bleached wood sunburst mirror also from the eighteenth century. The French limestone mantel was found at an antiques architectural elements shop in Houston called Chateau Domingue.

Accompanying her mother on buying trips to Europe for her mother's eponymous shop, Jane Moore Interiors, only confirmed her devotion to the Swedish aesthetic and started something of a family trend. "I was buying lots of English and French furniture at the time," remembers Jane, "but Shannon just zeroed in on the Swedish. Soon I was entranced by it as well!"

Shannon and her husband, Andrew, now reside in a 1930s home set among the leafy red oak trees of the Devonshire neighborhood in Dallas. Architect Frank Ryburn was brought in to redesign the upstairs space from two bedrooms with a large artist's studio to a living plan to accommodate a growing family. After a six-month renovation of the house, Shannon, like many an overwhelmed young mother before her, called upon her own mother from Houston to help with the project. "I was so lucky to have her! Our daughter, Susanna, had just been born and our son, Cooper, was in preschool," recalls Shannon. New baby in arms, Shannon would work on the project room by room with Jane. Both women knew that they wanted a Swedish aesthetic for this home and set about having the floors lightened. Window treatments were kept to a minimum, allowing the original floor-to-ceiling windows to stand out. "The most exciting part for me was choosing the Swedish furniture," says Shannon. "Each Swedish antique has a story to tell as you

examine the painted patina. Of course, these pieces also have special meaning for me as reminders of fantastic adventures and the time in Europe spent with my mom."

While Shannon's joy has been in furnishing the interior of the home, Andrew's enthusiasm has been in designing and installing the extensive gardens on the property. The Swedish concept of bringing the inside out and the outside in is fully realized by Andrew in a succession of boxwood parterre rooms linked by arbors, picket fences, and, most dramatically, by elephant-height painted gates from India. Espaliered vines act as lush tapestry wall hangings for the brick-enclosed kitchen terrace furnished with a faux bois dining table and chairs. Having grown up in Atlanta, Andrew decided to plant hydrangea and dogwood—no mean feat in Texas weather conditions. He remains undaunted and has even inaugurated a massive bed of ferns. A large screened porch, another ode to Andrew's Southern roots, has been put in place with grapevine chairs and a nineteenth-century French settee for lounging on, all the better to hear the flowing water fountains hidden in the nearby rose garden. The view into these evocative garden rooms through each window awakens a deep connection to nature while it imparts a wonderful sense of proportion about the whole property.

To say that Andrew and Shannon grew up in artistic households would be an understatement. Andrew's mother, Lisa Newsom, is the founder and editor-in-chief of *Veranda*, a premier design magazine; and Shannon's mother, mentioned earlier, is the highly regarded Houston-based interior designer Jane Moore. Where such interesting design lineages collide, surely inspiration is to follow. Shortly after their marriage, Shannon and Andrew founded Wisteria, a catalog of unique furnishings and accessories from around the world. "Many of the pieces that we have replicated are from the house," says Shannon, "and I work with craftsmen to get the look and feel just right." Quality design, she and Andrew feel, should be available to everyone. The couple's commitment to finding new and beautiful pieces for the catalog often takes them around the globe. However, when it comes to the Newsom's own nest, Sweden is a favorite influence. "When we come home," says Shannon, "we want a peaceful background where we can unwind, and the Swedish country style, with its muted color palette and soft, simple lines, does just that."

ABOVE: A pair of large-scale eighteenth-century French lanterns were the inspiration for those made for the Newsom's Wisteria catalog. A nineteenth-century oil-on-canvas of a Provence landscape hangs in the background.

FACING: Lemon rununculae and apricot roses make a splendid centerpiece on Shannon's French polished-steel dining table. An early nineteenth-century tall case Swedish clock with scraped and weathered patina provides weight and a focal point to a narrow wall. Note how a Swedish look is so easily achieved with a few Swedish elements. Shannon and Andrew always eat in the dining room with the children; the crisp white slipcovers are washable and protect the chair seats from little hands.

FACING: A large eighteenth-century Swedish tall case clock stands in front of a French eighteenth-century screen. The screen has a blue frame with oil-on-canvas painted panels of pastoral scenes from the French countryside, alternating with panels of flower bouquets in urns. An eighteenth-century painted blue armoire from France is dramatic as well as functional.

ABOVE: Soft French and Italian linens await in the elegant master bedroom. A decoratively painted eighteenth-century French demi-lune table holds white roses from the garden.

FACING: Shannon and Andrew had all-new bathrooms put in with bright white tile, Italian marble, and polished-nickel fixtures.

ABOVE: Susanna's bed curtains drape onto the pale blue-and-green antique Oushak rug in her bedroom. An eighteenth-century black armchair makes a stylish seat next to a nineteenth-century Swedish chest of drawers.

FACING: This blue-painted eighteenth-century French commode easily passes for a Swedish cousin. A French nineteenth-century herbier hangs on the wall above a French wrought-iron candleholder.

ABOVE: The screened-in porch makes a shady retreat and a great room for outdoor entertaining. The handmade grapevine chairs, glazed turquoise ceramic stools, and cotton dhurrie rug are all pieces from Wisteria.

FACING: A sweeping green lawn is shaded by majestic oak trees at the Newsom's Dallas residence.

ABOVE: This is one of the many entrances leading to various garden rooms on the property.

NORTHERN TREASURE CHEST

THE HUDSON VALLEY RETREAT OF MARIANNE THORSÉN

Screenwriter Dewitt Bodeen once remarked, "I like to see a home like this, a home connected with people's thoughts and work, and things they love." He would, most surely, have loved Marianne Thorsén's unrepentantly personal retreat overlooking Roundtop Mountain in upstate New York. The house is an atmospheric treasure chest filled with the evidence of Marianne's quintessentially Swedish life lived in America. Marianne had moved from Sweden to Manhattan when she was young, and soon, like many a successful New Yorker, she longed for a weekend retreat away from the city and her demanding real estate practice. She imagined a place to put up her feet, walk, and cook, to entertain friends, to garden, or—better yet—to just not answer the phone. As a realtor, Marianne had had her finger on the pulse of the Hudson Valley market for a long time but had not been able to find the right house to buy for herself. The exact day she found the house in Germantown is etched in her memory. "It was raining, and we came down the hill and there it was," she reminisces, "just like in Sweden with all of the outbuildings and a place for a Swedish flag."

FACING: The dining table was salvaged roadside and painted white. Ever practical, Marianne Thorsén has taken many a thrift store or roadside furniture find and breathed new life and use into it with paint and fabric.

LEFT: Swedish flagpoles resplendent with blue-and-yellow pennants are a common sight along the Swedish archipelago. Here, the Swedish flag is proudly waved over American soil.

The farmhouse with outbuildings is an ideal that runs deep in the Swedish psyche. Families will pass down their summerhouses—usually located on the archipelago, seashore, or overlooking a lake—from generation to generation. This house in New York was built in 1710 and the family who last owned it had left it much as it had been. The original front room had served as a meetinghouse. Everything about the property reminded Marianne of a typical Swedish summer compound in that there were wonderful outbuildings. There was a barn from the late nineteenth century, a garage, a shed, and a little three-seat outhouse—all with stunning views of the Catskills across the Hudson. The realtor was sold.

Marianne soon realized, to her surprise, that her house had a serious case of osteoporosis: the walls were being held up by nothing more than wallpaper! She quickly found herself up to her neck in renovations. Everything had to be taken down to the lath. But, thanks to her determination and dedication, a remarkable restoration job was done to preserve the antique quality of the house while still modernizing it. The dining room

is a key example of the care Marianne put into each room. She laboriously hand sanded the original floorboards and pickled them herself, adding blue and gray to the stain to bring more life to the wood. She put up new walls and tried six different layers of paint before settling on the soft green of the dining room. She brought down the dado to a color of her liking and decided to keep it. Marianne then painted the walls of the dining room in a stripe with quince blossoms based on a Swedish Långholmen documentary fabric sample. The pure provincial

FACING: Marianne had a Swedish ceramic stove or *kakelugn* installed in a corner of the dining room.

ABOVE LEFT: This rococo clock from 1740 was japanned at the turn of the nineteenth century, as was the fashion. The plates on either side of the clock are Chinese nineteenth century and from Marianne's extensive collection.

ABOVE RIGHT: This medicine chest of Gustav Adolfus II, Sweden's great warrior king, was given to Marianne's father, who was a surgeon, as a gift from a grateful patient. The seventeenth-century surgical instruments in the case are still so sharp that upon inspecting one, Marianne's father sliced his finger so badly that he could not operate the next day. A letter of provenance is framed next to the case.

When asked about which Swedish design influence inspired her choices in this home, Marianne answers very practically. "I am Swedish. My taste is not American. I did not even think when decorating this house 'Oh, this is not Swedish enough.' No, everything here is what pleases me. Certainly, though, being Swedish has influenced my taste," she says, pointing to the blue-and-yellow pennant rippling in the wind. "You can't have a house in the country without a Swedish flagpole!"

FACING: Marianne had a Swedish stove installed to heat the guesthouse. Wood-burning Swedish stoves are incredibly energy efficient and a perfect solution for heating a small building.

ABOVE: Rather than not have a dining area, Marianne opted to put a very narrow dining table in the entrance to the guesthouse. Cheery white-and-beige-checked fabric and white trim brighten the room and make it feel fresh.

RIGHT: Marianne loves to cook, and her guesthouse/bed-and-breakfast is fitted out with an inviting orange kitchen.

FACING: Here is Marianne Thorsén's Hudson River Valley farmhouse as viewed from the south. The glassed-in sleeping porch on the second story has breathtaking views of the river and Roundtop Mountain in the distance. Marianne installed the terrace, a cutting garden, a berry garden, and an eighty-foot-long garden bed.

ABOVE: The outhouse has been converted to a cheerful red-and-yellow garden shed. Garden sheds like these can be found throughout Sweden, where even apartment dwellers have their own gardening plots with storage sheds.

A SWEDISH COUNTRY RETREAT

THE CONNECTICUT HOME OF PEGGY AND KEITH ANDERSON

While spending summers in Connecticut, Peggy and Keith Anderson stumbled upon a 1760 New England farmhouse in the hills of Litchfield County. The house was reminiscent of Peggy's grandparents' home in the Swedish province of Småland, where she spent every summer as a child, and Peggy felt drawn to the location because of its beauty and familiarity.

FACING: By combining modern furniture and accessories with traditional Swedish furniture, Peggy has created a sophisticated and elegant living room. The lack of heavy drapery throughout the house allows for daylight to illuminate the interior spaces.

LEFT: The beauty of Swedish neutrals is in the blending of textures and materials, highlighted by bold colors for balance. Peggy has accomplished this by using a pale palette for her settee and wall treatment and then adding two Chinese celadon urns and a painting she inherited from her grandparents of a fort in Varberg, Sweden. The painting, which has all the color elements of the floor, urns, and settee, works as a wonderful balance for the room. This creates interest and movement rather than a stagnant space.

Residents of Manhattan during the workweek, the Andersons wanted a country house where they could escape on weekends and raise their family. The Connecticut house seemed perfect for just that. Having inherited several period antiques and paintings from her grandparents, Peggy relished the idea of being able to finally find a home for them that would be a perfect fit. Peggy says, "I inherited lots of knickknacks, Christmas ornaments, tea cups, silver, books, linens, tea towels, and so on—stuff that might seem a bit kitschy or ornamental elsewhere, but what I found is that they give my house a soul."

Peggy's design approach has changed over the course of the ten years since the Andersons first acquired the property. Originally a bit more colorful, her direction has evolved, bringing her closer to her Swedish roots. She has removed color from her interior palette and instead introduced grays and shades of white as her primary color scheme. Establishing neutrals as a base, she then adds hints of color by means of her accessories, leaving the key elements in the room neutral.

According to Peggy, "Originally the interiors were more contrived to look Swedish, and when I pared down things (to the pale grays and whites), it allowed the house to become more authentic in its owner's heritage, still with a nod to the 1760 structure. I really feel like my house has a soul. That it is a sanctuary for these family heirlooms that could have been packed away or lost. I do feel more spiritually connected to my past and heritage when I am here."

Peggy's sophisticated style is very apparent in her ability and confidence to mix modern furniture with period antiques. Not limiting herself, Peggy's love for Scandinavian modern furniture as well as antiques has inspired her to pepper the house with key modern pieces. Truly Scandinavian, this design approach is both fresh and exciting. "The modern furniture is a way to balance everything," she says. For example, the kitchen chairs are from IKEA, and the table is a nineteenth-century Swedish trestle farm table. Keeping in mind that the clean, almost modern lines of most Swedish-period antiques sit beautifully with twentieth-century modern designs, the natural progression is a marriage of both.

The house has been and continues to be a vital part of the Andersons' family life. Summers are busy with activity, and winters are a time of celebration, when Swedish traditions are shared. Peggy's favorite time of year is around the holidays, when the festivities she knew as a child are passed down to her children. "They would never want to spend Christmas anywhere else. They love all that stuff, and I think that this is a gift to my children." Swedish tree trimming, baking ginger cookies, and mulling the secret family glug recipe are especially rewarding. Knowing that these traditions will continue to the next generation in the same special way that made it such a treasured memory for Peggy is ultimately what the Andersons wanted to achieve with their house in the country.

Incorporating a nineteenth-century Swedish pine trestle table with reproduction Swedish IKEA bellman chairs, Peggy has created a beautiful yet functional family-friendly kitchen. Blue-and-white homespun fabrics are introduced to add color and highlight the space. Traditional Swedish roll blinds are the only colored window treatments in the house. Because this room is so sunny, Peggy's use of color in no way detracts from inviting light into the space. Instead, it acts as a grounding force in the room. The light fixture suspended above the trestle table is the "PH5" by designer Poul Henningsen.

ABOVE: The long, dark winters of Sweden seem to go on forever, until the first shoots of spring flowers appear and a scent of sweet spring is in the air. That feeling of happiness and renewal is vital to Swedish interiors. Sunlight is cherished; nature is respected. In this room, the warm woods of the French farm table and the American wide-plank floors complement the coolness of the painted antique baroque chairs, sparse window treatments, and painted walls. The combination of wood, paint, and light reflect nature with a pure elegance that is calming and not contrived.

FACING: Soft colors highlighted by splashes of vibrant colors once again help to merge the modern with the traditional. The pillows are from the traditional line of Swedish Svensk Tenn fabrics designed by Joseph Frank.

FACING: Health and well-being are an integral part of Scandinavian living. The sauna assists the body in ridding itself of toxins while increasing circulation.

ABOVE: Interior and exterior spaces become one, highlighted by interior wood surfaces and spacious windows. Suspended above the tub is a "snowball" pendant light fixture designed by Poul Henningsen (1894–1967).

ABOVE: Historically, built-in beds served a functional purpose more than a decorative one. The enclosed walls of the built-ins (usually facing the hearth in the main living room) retained heat and were reserved for the older members of the family. Towards the end of the eighteenth century, these beds became highly decorative, thanks mainly to the traveling apprentice artists who had been trained at the court of Gustav III. Today, when we think of a Swedish country bed, the painted built-in bed comes to mind.

RIGHT: Crisp linens, simple window treatments, and highlights of navy create an elegant, spacious, and inviting master bedroom.

DAWN HILL ANTIQUES

THE SHOP OF PAULETTE AND JOHN PEDEN

ℒocated in the bucolic rolling hills of Litchfield County, Connecticut, Dawn Hill Antiques is a destination for anyone interested in the decorative arts. Established sixteen years ago and located in the original post office and market building of New Preston, Connecticut, Dawn Hill Antiques (named after the street, Dawn Hill Road, where the Pedens live), specializes in eighteenth- and nineteenth-century Swedish antiques with an emphasis on original painted surfaces.

FACING: The Swedish Slag Bord, or drop-leaf table, represents a classic form in both antique and contemporary Swedish furniture design. The Slag Bord is such an important part of Swedish lifestyle living, and yet it is so simple. Historically, the Slag Bord was found in rooms that were used for entertaining. During festive times, they were pulled out and extended to work as harvest tables. During quiet times, perhaps only one leaf was extended, allowing the user to work on the space without having to pull the table completely away from the wall. The table was simply left along the side of the wall waiting for the next event. Almost every Swedish home in the eighteenth and nineteenth centuries had one form or another of the Slag Bord.

LEFT: Located in the historic village of New Preston, Connecticut, Dawn Hill Antiques is a treasure trove of eighteenth- and nineteenth-century Swedish and European antiques.

While traveling through Europe almost twenty years ago, John and Paulette Peden (a photographer and a marketing executive) found that they had collected quite a few antiques during their journey. As a hobby, they decided to open a shop specializing in blue-and-white transferware. Soon, the business expanded to also include French-painted furniture and garden antiques. With the success of the business established, a hobby turned into a serious venture. John and Paulette called upon Jane Fredrikson to help them manage the store. Jane, originally born in Stockholm and raised in Malmo, Sweden, joined the team, and the natural progression to Swedish Antiques began. According to Jane, whose memories of her childhood in Sweden are filled with wonderful antiques that were passed down for generations, "The Swedish style took inspiration from the French; it is pared down and more restrained, focusing on pale colors and simple lines. Swedish interiors are decorated but the look is clean and uncluttered."

The Pedens were ready for a new direction for their store, and it was Paulette's love of a Swedish tall case clock that finally catapulted them into collecting fine Swedish antiques of the Gustavian and rococo periods. Paulette was inspired by the soft palette, the intriguing textures of two-hundred-year-old paint surfaces, and a pared-down aesthetic that was classical but could also relate to modern design. The simple placement of a great Swedish chair or clock, she found, could set the mood and transform an entire room.

When the Pedens bought the building, it needed some renovation, but the high ceilings and spacious sunlit rooms were ideal for presenting period Swedish furnishings. Paulette, excited by the new direction, took inspiration from the manor homes in Sweden that she had visited, and designed the interior of the store in pale white-washed colors to reflect a calm and beautiful world to walk into. Her desire was to "create a mood of tranquility and elegance where all the elements of living graciously are represented." As a result, when you walk into Dawn Hill Antiques, one feels transported to a manor house in eighteenth-century Gustavian Sweden. In fact, during the darker months, Jane even lights candles throughout the store, creating a welcoming glow that is reminiscent of Sweden in winter.

FACING: When the Pedens moved Dawn Hill Antiques to its existing space, Paulette took the opportunity to truly transform the interiors, thus creating a Gustavian-inspired mood. Grays, creams, and blues create a soothing color palette along with the decorative "diamond" motif floor painting which was inspired by many of the historic manor homes in Sweden. The effect was to create the look of a stone slab floor, adding depth and interest to what would ordinarily just be finished wood flooring.

ABOVE: Fine eighteenth- and nineteenth-century Swedish antiques compose a beautiful space in the garden room highlighted by nineteenth-century garden elements and English ironstone and transfer ware.

LEFT: A beautifully carved and rare Bornholm Clock (from the Danish island of Bornholm, located between Sweden and Denmark) stands proudly side by side an eighteenth-century Swedish rococo glass-front armoire.

FACING: Antique blue-and-white English transfer ware is the inspiration for the studio kitchen. In keeping with Swedish love of symmetry, the backsplash motif reflects the china displayed above. Soft blue hues are applied to the cabinetry to complement the blue tones in the transfer ware, subtle gray marble grounds the countertops and balances out the stainless steel appliances. A winter white porcelain sink acts in concert with the backsplash.

ACKNOWLEDGMENTS

To Jon Monson and Buffer Ergmann, whose dedication and fresh eyes kept us inspired. Thank you both for a second go around, your photography, and another beautiful book!

To Lisa Newsom and David Easton for their love of Swedish design, graciousness, and heartfelt forewords—we are honored.

To Gibbs Smith, book designers Sheryl Dickert Smith and Maralee Nelson, and our favorite editor, Jennifer Grillone. We love working with all of you! Thank you.

We especially wish to thank the following individuals and institutions for their invaluable guidance, graciousness, insight, time, and shelter: Lisa Segalis, Peter Dixon and Gary Brewer of Richard A. M. Stern Architects, Per and Miriam Ralamb, Kathy and Bruce Carlsted, The Minnesota Historical Museum, photographer Peter Aarons and Christine Codanzzo at Esto Agency, Yola and Nick Mourginis, Woodstock Artists Association, The James Cox Gallery, Nena Thurman and the Menla Mountain Retreat.

Thank you to the homeowners and designers whose work appears here in our chapters. You opened your homes and projects to us and we thank you for sharing your love of Swedish design with our readers—this book is yours.

We would like to thank our amazing team at Eleish van Breems. Thank you to Jamie Arber for handling the insanity of our lives! You have added so much to Eleish van Breems. Thank you to Pedro Guerra for creating such beautiful finishes and to Jane Edwards and Shelly Miller for your charming presence and elegance. Thanks to our patient bookkeeper Laurie for making sense of it all.

Thank you to all of our friends for your love and support with special shout outs on this book to: Melinda Monson, Kristen and Charlie Allen, Peggy Anderson, Denise Adams (from the beginning), Cynthia Baber, Diana Beattie, Ester den Breems, Gwen den Breems, Dianne Bernhard, David Boughner, Ralph D'Aniello, Patty and Chris Clark, Mike Dworkin, Liz and David Frassinelli, Anne Gobran, Sue Kring, Julia (Webber), Steve and Esme Taylor, the Austin Family, Sheraton Kalouria, David Ganak and Jim Sargent, S. Ganesha, Carmela Greco, Ingrid and Rich Gordon and family, Peter Germaine, Bruce and Lisa Miller, Christine Murphy, Mary Muryn, Ryan Rosano, Alan Spirer, Angela Thomas, Tim Tareco, Hezekiah Thompson, Dechen Thurman, Kathleen Spinelli from Brands to Books, Philip Stone and Robert Admansky, Caroline Weidemann, Rosemary Williams and Diane Yarrow.

Rhonda particularly wishes to thank: my wonderful parents, Cathy and G. Eleish and to Van and Dianne Bernhard, and Diane and Harrison Valante cheerleaders for all things EVBA! Thank you to my loving daughter and my pride and joy, Kari Eleish Ergmann. Thank you also to my family: My sister, P. Eleish and family, the Elliott family, and the Dittus family. Zan Congrats, and Matt, welcome to the family! Thank you to my family in Sweden: My Aunt Ittan Gullers Causbie, Ingvor Gullers, Suzanne (I love you and be in peace), Karin, Sergio, Alexa and Meg. Thank you to my family in France: My Aunt Sally Lenoir and family. Thank you to Nick and Yola Mourginis (my other parents) and David Ganak (a blessing in my life), Ariana Ganak and Jim Sargent.

Edie particularly wishes to thank: my parents, Diane and Harrison Valante and Van and Dianne Bernhard thank you for all of your love and emotional support, now and always. You are my rocks and I love you. To my sisters and brothers, nieces and nephews and cousins, my admiration and love. Skal! To my other family Gamal and Cathy Eleish for your creative support. To Allyson Cosgrove and Lily for taking such wonderful care of life at Catamount. To Paul Esser, the in-house grammarian who I think is superlative in every way, all my love. Finally to my loving, brilliant sons Lars and Martin who let me do another book and are now working on ones of their own. I love you!

RESOURCE GUIDE

NORTHEAST

Antiques, Furnishings, and Accessories

Avolli, LLC
P.O. Box 2607
South Portland, ME 04116
207.767.1901

3 Southgate Road, Suite 1 and 2
Scarborough, ME 04074
207.767.1901
www.avolli.com
Scandinavian antique furniture

Clearly First
980 Madison Avenue
New York, NY 10021
212.988.8242
www.clearlyfirst.com

Dienst & Dotter
23 Bridge Street
Sag Harbor, NY 11963
631.725.6881
www.dienstanddotter.com

The Country Gallery
Antiques of Vermont
P.O. Box 70
1566 Route 315
Rupert, VT 05768
802.394.0076
www.country-gallery.com
Scandinavian pine antique furniture

Country Swedish
22 Elizabeth Street
South Norwalk, CT 06854
203.855.1106

979 Third Avenue, Suite 1409
New York, NY 10022
212.838.1976
www.countryswedish.com
Swedish reproduction furniture

Cupboards & Roses Swedish Antiques
296 South Main Street, Route 7
Sheffield, MA   01257
413.229.3070
www.cupboardsandroses.com
Eighteenth- and nineteenth-century painted furniture, especially Mora clocks and Scandinavian folk art

Dawn Hill Antiques
11 Main Street
New Preston, CT 06777
860.868.0066
www.dawnhillantiques.com
Dealing in fine eighteenth- and nineteenth-century Swedish antiques

Evergreen Antiques
1249 Third Avenue
New York, NY 10021
212.744.5664
www.evergreenantiques.com
Specializing in fine Scandinavian and Baltic antiques

Eleish van Breems, Ltd.
18 Titus Road
P.O. Box 313
Washington Depot, CT 06794
860.868.1200
www.evbantiques.com
A full-service Scandinavian Design Center offering the best Nordic design of past, present, and future, and featuring fine eighteenth- and nineteenth-century Swedish Gustavian antiques

G. Sergeant Antiques
88 Main Street North
Woodbury, CT 06798
203.266.4177
www.gsergeant.com
Period furnishings of English, American, Continental, and Asian origins

James Cox Gallery
4666 Route 212
Willow, NY 12495
845.679.7608
www.jamescoxgallery.com

Just Scandinavian
161 Hudson Street
New York, NY 10013
212.334.2556
www.justscandinavian.com
A selection of Svenskt Tenn textiles, furnishings, and accessories

Karl Kemp & Associates, Ltd.
36 East 10th Street
New York, NY 10003
212.254.1877

833 Madison Avenue
New York, NY 10021
212.288.3838
www.karlkemp.com
*Bierdermeier-, art deco–, and
empire-style antiques*

Lars Bolander
72 Gansevoort Street
(Between Washington Street
and 9th Avenue)
New York, NY 10014
212.924.1000
www.larsbolander.com
*A selection of Swedish antiques and
international furniture and accessories*

The Lenkoran Gallery
Buckingham Road
Brooklyn, NY 11226
212.655.9352
www.lenkoran.co.uk
*By appointment only
Antique rugs and textiles*

Next Step Antiques
199 Ethan Allen Highway (Rt. 7)
Ridgefield, CT 06877
203.431.8083
www.nextstepantiques.com
A selection of Scandinavian antiques

Real Gustavian
389 Stockbridge Road
Great Barrington, MA 01230
413.528.4440
www.realgustavian.com
Specializing in Swedish Gustavian antiques

Tone on Tone
7920 Woodmont Avenue
Bethesda, MD 20814
240.497.0800
www.tone-on-tone.com

White On White
200 Lexington Avenue, Suite 715
New York, NY 10021
212.988.9194
www.whiteonwhiteny.com

Cultural Organizations
The American Scandinavian
Foundation Scandinavia House
The Nordic Center in America
58 Park Avenue
New York, NY 10016
212.879.9779
www.scandinaviahouse.org

The Woodstock Artists
Association & Museum
28 Tinker Street
Woodstock, NY 12498
845.679.2198
www.woodstockart.org

Restaurants
Restaurant Aquavit of New York
65 East 55th Street
New York, NY 10022
212.307.7311
www.aquavit.org

Appraisal Services
L. George Walker Appraisals
Jane Edwards
315 Hulls Hill Road
Southbury, CT 06488
203.264.5548
lgeorgewalker@earthlink.net
*Appraisals of Swedish decorative and fine art
for insurance, resale, and estate purposes*

MIDWEST

Antiques, Furnishings,
and Accessories
Blondell Antiques
Tom and Doris Blondell
1406 2nd Street S.W.
Rochester, MN 55902
507.282.1872
www.blondell.com
*A selection of eighteenth- and nineteenth-
century Swedish country antiques*

Ericson Gallery
P.O. Box 12212
Des Moines, IA 50312
515.279.0591
www.ericsongallery.com
*Scandinavian folk art, Nordic textiles,
weavings, quilts, and metal ware*

Nordic Style
1005 North Commons Drive
Aurora, IL 60504
630.851.2111
www.nordicstyle.com
Classic Swedish furniture and accessories

Midnight Sun Antiques
110 West Lake Street
Libertyville, IL 60048
847.362.5240
www.midnightsunantiques.com
Swedish antiques and vintage furniture

Country Swedish
1621 Merchandise Mart
Chicago, IL 60654
312.644.4540
www.countryswedish.com

Cultural Organizations
The American Swedish Institute
2600 Park Avenue South
Minneapolis, MN 55407
612.871.4907
www.americanswedishinst.org

Swedish American Museum Center
5211 North Clark Street
Chicago, IL 60640
773.728.8111
www.samac.org

Ten Chimneys Foundation
P.O. Box 225
S43 W31575 Depot Road
Genesee Depot, WI 53127
262.968.4161
Tour Reservation Line:
262.968.4110, ext. 211
www.tenchimneys.org

MID-ATLANTIC

Antiques, Furnishings, and
Accessories
Choate & Von Z.
6635 Paxson Road
Solebury, PA 18963
215.297.5287
www.choateandvonz.com
*Eighteenth- and nineteenth-century
Swedish antiques*

Klaradal Swedish Antiques & Furnishings
16644 Georgia Avenue
Olney, MD 20832
301.570.2557
www.klaradal.com

Svenska Mobler
154 North La Brea Avenue
Los Angeles, CA 90036
323.934.4452
www.svenskamobler.com

Cultural Organizations
American Swedish Historical Museum
1900 Pattison Avenue
Philadelphia, PA 19145
215.389.1776
www.americanswedish.org

SOUTHERN

Antiques, Furnishings,
and Accessories
A. Tyner Antique
200 Bennett Street, NW
Atlanta, GA 30309
404.367.4484
www.swedishantiques.biz
European and Swedish antiques

Joli International
7878 Roswell Road, Suite 300
Atlanta, GA 30350
405.259.9148
www.joliinternational.com

Swede Home
P.O. Box 460103
Ft. Lauderdale, FL 33346
954.829.6272
www.swedehomeantiques.com
Swedish antiques, furniture, and accessories

Lars Bolander
3731 South Dixie Highway
West Palm Beach, FL 33405
561.832.2121
www.larsbolander.com

Jane Moore Interiors
2922 Virginia Street
Houston, TX 77098
713.526.6113

WESTERN

Antiques, Furnishings,
and Accessories
Swedish Country Interiors
P.O. Box 14851
Tumwater, WA 98511
360.570.0876
www.swedishcountry.com

Swedish Room
Suzanna Havden Bell
Sobel Design Building
680 Eight Street, Suite 151
San Francisco, CA 94103
415.255.0154
www.swedishroom.com

Lief, Inc.
646 North Almont Drive
West Hollywood, CA 90069
310.492.0033
www.liefalmont.com

Swedish Heirlooms
2911 East Madison Street
Seattle, WA 98112
206.621.1002
www.swedishheirlooms.com
Swedish reproduction furniture

St Barths Home
303 Broadway
Suite 104–123
Laguna Beach, CA 92657
www.stbarthshome.com
800.274.9096
*A lifestyle concept store from the creators of
Swedish Blonde. Swedish home furnishings*

Cultural Organizations
Nordic Heritage Museum
3014 NW 67th Street
Seattle, WA 98117
206.789.5707
www.nordicmuseum.org

INTERIOR DESIGNERS

Cebolla Fine Flowers
Jamie Huizenga
4415 Lover's Lane
Dallas, TX 75225
214.369.7673

5610 Maple Avenue
Dallas, TX 75235
www.cebollafineflowers.com

James M. Chadwick
Landscape Architectural Design
1328 Millich Lane
San Jose, CA 95117
408.374.8657
chadwickhj@earthlink.net

Diana Beattie
Diana Beattie Interior Design
1136 – 5th Avenue
New York, NY 10128
212.722.6226
dianabeattieint@verizon.com

Rhonda Eleish
Eleish van Breems, Ltd.
18 Titus Road
P.O. Box 313
Washington Depot, CT 06794
860.868.1200
www.evbantiques.com
evba@evbantiques.com

Richard Hershner
917.536.8588

Derek Clarke
Architectural Designer
203.414.1837

Bruce Budd
165 East 65th Street
New York, NY 10021
212.737.5131

Libby Holsten
108 Poppasquash Road
Bristol, RI 02809
401.254.1006

Jane Moore Interiors
2922 Virginia Street
Houston, TX 77098
713.526.6113

Howard B. Post, Architect
430 Sherman Avenue, Suite 206
Palo Alto, CA 94306
650.328.6963
postarch@pacbell.net

Swedish Room
Suzanna Havden Bell
Sobel Design Building
680 Eight Street, Suite 151
San Francisco, CA 94103
415.255.0154
www.swedishroom.com